ALSO BY ABIGAIL KIRSCH

The Bride & Groom's First Cookbook
(with Susan M. Greenberg)

Invitation to Dinner
(with David Nussbaum)

BROADWAY BOOKS

New York

The Bride & Groom's Menu Cookbook

ABIGAIL KIRSCH

with Susan M. Greenberg

Broadway Books titles may be purchased for business or promotional use or for special sales. For information, please write to: Special Markets Department, Random House, Inc., 1540 Broadway, New York, NY 10036.

BROADWAY BOOKS and its logo, a letter B bisected on the diagonal, are trademarks of Broadway Books, a division of Random House, Inc.

Visit our website at www.broadwaybooks.com

Library of Congress Cataloging-in-Publication Data

Kirsch, Abigail.
    The bride & groom's menu cookbook / Abigail Kirsch, with Susan M. Greenberg.—1st ed.
      p. cm.
    Includes index.
    1. Dinners and dining. 2. Entertaining. 3. Menus. I. Greenberg, Susan M. II. Title.
TX737 .K58 2002
642'.4—dc21   2001035425

FIRST EDITION

PRINTED IN THE UNITED STATES OF AMERICA

Designed by Nancy Campana / Campana Design
Illustrated by Jill Weber / Frajil Farms Productions

ISBN 0-7679-0615-2

10 9 8 7 6 5 4 3 2 1

To all who enjoyed

The Bride & Groom's First Cookbook

and to the brides and grooms of the new millennium.

Table of Contents

Acknowledgments

OUR SPECIAL THANKS TO PAM BERNSTEIN, JENNIFER Josephy, and Judith Kern for their continued confidence in this project. We also want to acknowledge the kitchen team at Abigail Kirsch Culinary Productions, with special thanks to Alison Awerbuch, corporate executive chef; Kevin Garufi, for sharing his expertise in wine; and Fran Kelly, whose input in this manuscript was invaluable. Thanks also to Laura Geller.

The Bride & Groom's Menu Cookbook

Introduction

ENTERTAINING SHOULD BE A WONDERFUL EXPERIENCE for you and for your guests. It is fun and, yes, it is challenging. But don't be intimidated. Relax and enjoy cooking together, and your guests will also relax and enjoy themselves.

In *The Bride & Groom's First Cookbook,* we helped you get started with recipes from hors d'oeuvre to desserts. We also provided menus for special occasions. Now that you are adept at moving around the kitchen and working together, you are ready to entertain and share your delight and newly acquired skills in the culinary arts.

The menus in *The Bride & Groom's Menu Cookbook* are designed and arranged seasonally. Our palates change as we move from season to season, with an emphasis on hearty, stick-to-your-ribs food in the winter and a yen for charcoal-grilled entrées in the summer. The menus for each season are divided into five categories, featuring fish, poultry, meat, pasta, and vegetarian dishes. The variety is endless. Mix and match according to your taste. It always helps to be aware of any dietary concerns your guests might have—vegetarian, low-fat, food allergies—but it's not always possible to know about these restrictions in advance. Sometimes just maintaining a sense of humor is the key to success. On one memorable occasion we cooked a spectacular shellfish feast of shrimp, lobster, crabmeat, mussels, and clam chowder. One of our guests was highly allergic to shellfish. A quick omelet saved the day. The lesson to be learned? Be flexible!

The book is organized in the same easy-to-follow format as *The Bride & Groom's First Cookbook*. The recipes are not complicated. They're fun, and they reflect today's global cuisine. We've again used readily obtainable ingredients and provided "Cook's Tips" and preparation and cooking times, as well as a list of basic kitchenware you will need to gather before starting to cook. Most recipes also include "Do-Ahead" suggestions for the best ways to use your time (and energy). It's nice to know when you arrive home from work at 6:00 P.M. and your guests are expected at 7:00, that you've planned in advance and all the ingredients and cookware are waiting for you.

In today's fast-paced world, with modern transportation and refrigeration, most ingredients are on the shelves year-round. The difference is in the pricing and, in some instances, the quality. For example, you can serve blueberries and raspberries in January. But in the winter months, these special treats will cost twice as much as they do in the summer. Squash is another example. In the fall, it is in season. For a price, it is available in the spring. Quality can be a factor, too. Although hothouse tomatoes look beautiful, they are never as sweet and juicy as summer tomatoes.

Our menus have been created to take advantage of the freshest ingredients at the time of year when they are in their prime. On page 283, we provide a chart listing the seasonal availability of most produce to serve as a quick reference for the frugal cook.

There are wine recommendations to accompany each menu. Here, too, prices vary. Most neighborhood liquor stores have resident wine experts who are usually delighted to share their knowledge and suggest which Chardonnay, Cabernet, or Merlot is the current best buy. Talking with these enthusiasts is a wonderful way to acquire a basic education in pairing wines with foods.

Have fun, create a warm and welcoming ambiance for your guests, and your meal will be a smashing success.

A little creativity goes a long way toward producing a lovely, unique dinner. This is the time to bring out all those shower, engagement, and wedding gifts and to allow those "orphans"—dishes and bowls that match nothing else in your china cabinet—to shine. That black enamel tray on the top shelf is the perfect background for the Asian-Spiced Scallop Saté. The colorful Rhubarb and Strawberry Chutney will be a standout in the white embossed bowl your boss gave you. And those multicolored dishtowels that are still in their original wrapping will make wonderful oversize napkins for the Pulled-Pork Barbecue dinner.

Showing a flair for the unusual when you set your table will make your guests feel that you care enough to have created a special atmosphere. Try using candles of different sizes, shapes, and colors—orange and black candles at Halloween or yellow, lilac, and pink to accompany a spring menu. Find unusual napkin rings to add a festive air. Design simple centerpieces in flowerpots or a variety of baskets to reflect the season.

In the spring, when tulips, daffodils, and hyacinths are in bloom, collect vases of different heights, put a few blooms in each, and distribute them randomly along the table. For summer menus, beautiful fresh fruits placed in special bowls not only add a lovely seasonal touch to your table but also serve as dessert. Fall is squash time. Create a warm autumn feeling with baskets of yellow and green squash, gourds, and pumpkins—and then cook the squash for another meal.

Winter greens make lovely centerpieces, too. And the smell of pine needles adds a welcoming aroma to your room. Fill crystal bowls with multicolored holiday ornaments for a festive touch. Apples are available year-round and look lovely as table decorations.

Take a walk through Pier One; Crate and Barrel; Home Depot; Bed, Bath, and Beyond; Williams-Sonoma; Pottery Barn; Restoration Hardware; your menus, check for similar ingredients in more than one recipe. (For example, you can save time by chopping onions in advance for all the recipes that call for chopped onions.)

3. Select your serving dishes. If the meal is casual, pick up flowers or center-piece fruit. If it's a special occasion, plan a theme.

4. Buy wine or other beverages ahead of time.

5. Don't forget to wear aprons.

6. Work over wax paper or paper toweling to make cleanup as quick and easy as possible.

7. Always have a slightly damp towel nearby to wipe up spills on counters and range tops as they happen.

8. Clean and put away cookware and utensils as soon as you are finished using them.

9. Have your oven calibrated by a professional once a year.

10. Remember to preheat the oven when indicated in a recipe. A preheated oven should wait for you instead of your having to wait for it.

11. Dried herbs are more pungent than fresh ones. Use one-third to one-half the amount of a fresh herb.

12. After freezing prepared food, always reseason it to taste before serving.

CHAPTER 1

Mix-and-Match Hors d'Oeuvre

Asian-Spiced Scallop Saté

KITCHENWARE
medium bowl, wooden spoons, 18 wooden skewers (3 to 4 inches long), paper toweling, sharp paring knife, baking sheet, pastry brush

PREPARATION TIME
15 minutes

MARINATING TIME
2 to 3 hours

COOKING TIME
8 to 10 minutes

DO-AHEAD
Prepare through Step 4 up to 3 hours ahead.

1 teaspoon ground cumin
1 ½ teaspoons ground ginger
1 ½ teaspoons ground cinnamon
1 ½ teaspoons ground coriander
⅛ teaspoon cayenne
1 ½ teaspoons curry powder
2 teaspoons sugar
1 teaspoon salt
18 medium sea scallops, about 1 pound
1 recipe Asian Mustard Glaze (recipe follows)
Garnish: 1 bunch watercress, long stems removed

1. Preheat the oven to 350 degrees.

2. Blend the cumin, ginger, cinnamon, coriander, cayenne, curry powder, sugar, and salt together in the bowl with a wooden spoon.

3. Soak the skewers in cold water for 10 minutes, and dry them well with paper toweling.

4. Clean the scallops by stripping off the muscle that is attached to one side; use a sharp paring knife. Drop the scallops into the spice rub, tossing them with your fingers or two wooden spoons until they are entirely coated with the rub. Marinate in the refrigerator for 2 to 3 hours.

5. Thread one scallop onto the end of each wooden skewer. Arrange the skewers, ¾ inch apart, on the baking sheet. Roast the scallops 5 to 8 minutes, until they are opaque in the center.

SERVICE Brush the scallops with the warm Asian Mustard Glaze and arrange the skewers on a serving tray covered with a bed of watercress. Asian-Spiced Scallop Saté looks fantastic on a black enamel tray (omit the bed of watercress).

COOK'S TIP Substitute a meaty white fish such as halibut, cut into 1-inch-square pieces, for the scallops.

black pepper in the bowl with a metal spoon. Add the cooled shrimp, toss well, and marinate in the refrigerator for 4 to 6 hours. *(As the shrimp marinate, they get more garlicky.)*

SERVICE Drain the shrimp, reseason with additional salt and black pepper, and arrange them in a flat basket or on a black rectangular or round serving tray. Place the whole basil leaves in the center of the platter and serve with Ginger Yogurt Dip.

COOK'S TIP Sea scallops can be substituted for the shrimp. Heat 2 tablespoons of olive oil in a medium skillet over medium-high heat. Sear the scallops for 1 to 2 minutes on each side, until they are golden brown and opaque in the center when tested with the tip of a knife. Cut them in quarters and follow the instructions for the shrimp recipe.

Ginger Yogurt Dip

KITCHENWARE
small bowl, whisk

PREPARATION TIME
10 minutes

1 cup yogurt
1 teaspoon fresh lemon juice
½ teaspoon finely grated ginger
2 small cloves garlic, minced
Salt
Freshly ground pepper

Combine the yogurt, lemon juice, ginger, and garlic in the bowl. Add the salt and pepper to taste. Whisk well until the mixture is smooth.

SERVICE Place in a small bowl and serve with the Garlicky Doused Shrimp.

Gorgonzola and Caramelized Onion Tart

KITCHENWARE

chef's knife, large skillet, whisk, medium bowl, rack

PREPARATION TIME

20 minutes

COOKING TIME

1 hour

DO-AHEAD

If you plan to serve the tart at room temperature, bake it early in the day.

1 partially baked Savory Tart Shell (recipe follows)

2 tablespoons unsalted butter

2 tablespoons extra virgin olive oil or 2 tablespoons pancetta fat reserved from tart shell

1 large onion, chopped medium

¼ teaspoon salt

½ teaspoon sugar

2 large eggs, beaten

1¼ cups heavy cream or half-and-half

4 ounces Gorgonzola cheese, finely crumbled

Garnish: 1 bunch fresh flat-leaf parsley, washed, tough stems removed

1. Make and partially bake the Savory Tart Shell.

2. Preheat the oven to 375 degrees.

3. Heat the butter and oil (or reserved pancetta fat) in the skillet over medium heat. Add the onion, salt, and sugar and cook, stirring frequently, until the onion is golden brown and caramelized, 15 to 20 minutes. Cool slightly and evenly distribute in the bottom of the partially baked Savory Tart Shell.

4. Whisk the eggs, cream, and Gorgonzola together in the bowl until the mixture is well blended.

5. Pour the custard over the onion and bake the tart for 30 to 40 minutes, until a knife inserted in the center comes out clean. Transfer the tart to a cooling rack for 10 minutes.

SERVICE Cut the tart into 12 wedges and arrange them on a large round or rectangular platter. Decorate the platter with the flat-leaf parsley. This hors d'oeuvre requires small plates and forks.

COOK'S TIP The tart is excellent served at room temperature. Bake it ahead and let it wait for your guests.

Savory Tart Shell

KITCHENWARE

chef's knife, grater, medium
skillet, slotted spoon, paper
toweling, 2 medium bowls,
pastry cutter, food processor
(optional), wax paper or
aluminum foil, rolling pin, 9- or
10-inch fluted tart pan with a
removable bottom, sharp
knife, rack

PREPARATION
TIME

20 minutes

COOKING TIME

35 minutes

DO-AHEAD

The dough can be kept in the
refrigerator for 1 to 2 days
or stored in the freezer for up
to 2 months. The tart shell can
be baked early in the day it will
be served.

$\frac{1}{4}$ pound pancetta, finely chopped

1 cup all-purpose flour

$\frac{1}{4}$ cup finely grated Asiago cheese (1 ounce)

4 tablespoons ($\frac{1}{2}$ stick) unsalted butter, chilled, cut into
$\frac{1}{2}$-inch pieces

2 ounces cream cheese, chilled, cut into $\frac{1}{2}$-inch pieces

1 cup dried beans

1. Cook the pancetta in the skillet over medium heat until it
   is golden brown and crisp, about 20 minutes. Use a slotted
   spoon to transfer it to a paper towel–lined bowl to drain.
   Reserve the fat in the pan for the filling, if desired.

2. Choose either mixing method.

   By Hand: Combine the flour, pancetta, and Asiago in
   the other bowl. Cut in the butter and cream cheese
   with a pastry cutter or cool fingertips until the mixture
   looks like coarse floury granules. Sprinkle 1 $\frac{1}{2}$ to 2
   tablespoons cold water over the dough and mix lightly
   with your hands until you can gather it into a ball. If
   the dough feels moist and sticky, lightly flour your
   hands.

   Food Processor Method: Place the flour in the bowl of
   the food processor fitted with the steel blade. Add the
   butter and cream cheese. Pulse for 45 to 60 seconds,
   until the mixture resembles coarse meal. Add the
   pancetta and Asiago and pulse for 15 to 20 seconds more.

Place the dough in a bowl, add 1 tablespoon of water at a time, and mix it gently with a fork. Add more water as necessary until the dough can be pressed into a ball.

3. Wrap the dough in wax paper or aluminum foil and refrigerate it for 30 minutes.

4. Preheat the oven to 425 degrees.

5. Lightly flour a wooden board or work surface and a rolling pin. Roll the pastry lightly with the rolling pin, from the center outward in all directions, until it is $\frac{1}{8}$ inch thick and 2 inches larger than the rim of the tart pan.

6. Lightly flour the rolling pin. Pick up one edge of the pastry and roll it loosely around the rolling pin. Lift the rolling pin to the edge of the tart pan and unroll the pastry into the pan. Fit the dough snugly into the bottom of the pan. Using your thumbs, push upward along the sides of the pan. Press the dough into the scalloped ridges of the tart pan. Cut any excess pastry off the edge with a sharp knife.

7. To partially bake the crust, prick the bottom and sides with a fork, cover the bottom with aluminum foil, and weight the entire surface with the dried beans. Bake the crust for 8 to 10 minutes; remove the foil with the beans, and bake the shell for 2 minutes more. Transfer the shell to a rack to cool.

Green Gazpacho Shots

KITCHENWARE
chef's knife, small bowl,
wooden spoon, food processor
or blender, large bowl, 20 shot
glasses

PREPARATION
TIME
30 minutes

DO-AHEAD
Prepare the shots in the
morning and store them,
covered, in the refrigerator.

1 tablespoon fresh lime juice

2 tablespoons rice vinegar

¼ cup extra virgin olive oil

2 tablespoons fresh cilantro

1 teaspoon ground cumin

1 small zucchini, trimmed and coarsely chopped

2 tomatillos, husks removed, quartered

1 medium green bell pepper, cored, seeded,
  and coarsely chopped

1 medium cucumber, peeled, seeded, and coarsely chopped

1 small red onion, coarsely chopped

2 medium-ripe green tomatoes, coarsely chopped

¼ to ½ cup vegetable broth

Tabasco sauce

Salt

Garnish: ⅓ cup sour cream

1 bunch fresh cilantro, washed and trimmed

1. Blend the lime juice, vinegar, oil, cilantro leaves, and
   cumin in the small bowl with a wooden spoon.

2. Place the zucchini, tomatillos, bell pepper, cucumber,
   onion, and green tomatoes in batches in the bowl of the
   food processor fitted with the steel blade. Process, adding
   the lime juice mixture, 2 tablespoons at a time, to prevent
   the blade from being clogged with the vegetables. The

soup should have a crunchy texture; do not purée the vegetables. Pour the soup into the large bowl as each batch is processed.

3. When all the vegetables have been processed, add just enough vegetable broth to give the gazpacho a smoother consistency. Season the soup with the Tabasco sauce and salt to taste.

4. Refrigerate, covered, for 2½ to 3 hours before serving.

SERVICE Fill the shot glasses three-quarters full with the gazpacho. Top each glass with a dollop of sour cream. Arrange the glasses on a large tray, with the bunch of cilantro in the center. Guests can help themselves.

COOK'S TIP Pour the soup into a thermos and enjoy it during an afternoon of tailgating, at a picnic, or for a beach party.

Grilled Meatballs with Indian-Spiced Yogurt Sauce

KITCHENWARE

chef's knife, pepper mill, large bowl, pastry brush, baking sheet

PREPARATION TIME

30 minutes

COOKING TIME

6 minutes

DO-AHEAD

The meatballs can be formed early in the day, covered, and refrigerated.

2 pounds ground beef round

1 large red onion, minced

2 large cloves garlic

3 tablespoons light soy sauce

2 large eggs, beaten

¾ teaspoon minced ginger

¾ teaspoon salt

½ teaspoon freshly ground pepper

4 teaspoons extra virgin olive oil

1 recipe Indian-Spiced Yogurt Sauce (recipe follows)

Garnish: 2 tablespoons minced curly parsley

1. Combine the ground beef, onion, garlic, soy sauce, eggs, ginger, salt, and pepper in the bowl. Mix the ingredients with your hands until they are well blended and hold together well.

2. Preheat the broiler.

3. Brush the baking sheet with 2 teaspoons of the oil. With your hands, form the meat mixture into 24 round balls and place them 1½ inches apart on the baking sheet. *(Each ball should weigh about ½ ounce.)* Lightly moisten

your hands before forming each ball to facilitate rolling. Brush the meatballs with the remaining oil and broil them, 4 inches from the heating element, 6 to 8 minutes, turning them once, until they are cooked through.

SERVICE Place the meatballs in a shallow bowl with the Indian-Spiced Yogurt Sauce on the side, or cut off the top of a small round loaf of bread, remove the insides, and spoon the meatballs into the bread. Dust with chopped parsley for color.

Indian-Spiced Yogurt Sauce

KITCHENWARE
medium strainer, cheesecloth,
2 medium bowls, chef's knife,
pepper mill

PREPARATION TIME
10 minutes (does not include draining time for yogurt)

DO-AHEAD
The sauce can be made up to 3 days in advance. Store it, covered, in the refrigerator.

1 pint yogurt
2 medium cloves garlic, minced
1 tablespoon fresh lemon juice
2 tablespoons extra virgin olive oil
2 teaspoons ground cumin
2 teaspoons ground turmeric
¼ teaspoon cayenne
Salt and freshly ground pepper

1. Line the strainer with the cheesecloth. Place it over a bowl and spoon the yogurt into the strainer. Allow the yogurt to drain in the refrigerator for 3 hours.

2. Transfer the drained yogurt from the cheesecloth to the other bowl and blend in the garlic, lemon juice, oil, cumin, turmeric, and cayenne. Season to taste with salt and black pepper.

SERVICE Spoon the yogurt sauce into a bowl and serve it with the Grilled Meatballs.

COOK'S TIP This sauce also adds a spicy dimension to grilled fish and lamb.

Honey-Glazed Chicken Wings

KITCHENWARE

grater, chef's knife, large bowl, plastic wrap, 2 large baking sheets, aluminum foil

PREPARATION TIME

10 minutes

MARINATING TIME

1 to 2 hours

COOKING TIME

30 minutes

DO-AHEAD

The chicken wings can be marinated in the refrigerator for up to 2 days. Make sure to bring them to room temperature before baking.

½ cup fresh orange juice
½ cup pineapple juice
1 tablespoon orange zest
3 large cloves garlic, minced
¼ cup soy sauce
½ cup honey
1 tablespoon finely minced ginger
3 pounds plump chicken wings, tips removed,
  wings cut in half
Salt and freshly ground pepper
Garnish: 1 large lime, quartered

1. Combine the orange juice, pineapple juice, orange zest, garlic, soy sauce, honey, and ginger in the bowl. Add the chicken wings and toss until well coated with the marinade. Cover with plastic wrap and refrigerate for 1 to 2 hours.

2. Preheat the oven to 400 degrees. Line the baking sheets with aluminum foil.

3. Remove the wings from the marinade and place them 1 inch apart on the baking sheets. Bake for 20 minutes. Turn them over and bake for about 10 minutes more, until they are cooked through and golden brown.

SERVICE Arrange the chicken wings on a large decorative platter garnished with the lime wedges.

COOK'S TIPS Have plenty of paper napkins available for your guests. A few moist towelettes will be most welcome, too. For a stronger punch, add $\frac{1}{4}$ teaspoon of cayenne to the marinade.

Miniature Eggplant Crisps

KITCHENWARE
grater, food processor, pepper
mill, medium bowl, whisk,
2 large bowls, chef's knife,
slotted spoon, 2 baking sheets,
medium sauté pan with 2- to
2½-inch sides, deep-fat
thermometer,
paper toweling

**PREPARATION
TIME**
30 minutes

COOKING TIME
30 minutes

DO-AHEAD
Make the bread crumbs and
grate the cheese the day
before. The eggplant can be
prepared early in the day and
recrisped in a 350-degree oven
before serving.

2 slices white or sourdough bread (crusts trimmed)
½ cup all-purpose flour
1¼ teaspoons salt
¼ teaspoon freshly ground pepper
3 eggs
1 tablespoon milk
¾ cup freshly grated Parmesan cheese
¼ teaspoon cayenne
1 Japanese eggplant or 2 long zucchini equal
   to length of eggplant
1 cup vegetable oil
Garnish: 4 ounces chèvre cheese
1 small red bell pepper, cored, seeded, and finely diced

1. Put the slices of bread in the bowl of the food processor
   fitted with the steel blade and pulse until the bread
   becomes small soft crumbs. (*Do not overprocess the bread
   or it will become pasty and unusable.*) You should have
   ¾ cup of crumbs.

2. Combine the flour with ¾ teaspoon of the salt and the
   black pepper in the medium bowl.

3. Whisk the eggs with the milk in a large bowl and set
   aside.

4. Blend the bread crumbs with the Parmesan, the remaining ½ teaspoon of salt, and the cayenne in the other large
   bowl.

5. Trim and slice the eggplant into 25 to 30 rounds about ⅛ inch thick.

6. Toss the eggplant with the seasoned flour, shaking off the excess, and drop the slices, in batches, into the egg mixture. Remove the eggplant with a slotted spoon and toss it, again in batches, with the bread crumbs, coating it well on all sides. Arrange the breaded eggplant on a baking sheet.

7. Heat the oil in the sauté pan until the temperature has reached 375 degrees. Fry the eggplant in batches until it is golden on both sides, 2 to 3 minutes, and transfer it to a paper towel–lined baking sheet.

SERVICE   With the tip of a teaspoon or a piping bag, drop a small dollop of chèvre in the center of each eggplant slice. Finish the garnish with a pinch of diced red pepper in the center of the cheese, and arrange the crisps on a colorful hors d'oeuvre tray. Serve the crisps warm.

COOK'S TIP   Mix eggplant and zucchini crisps for variety.

Prosciutto Tortilla Roulades with Dried Fig Jam

KITCHENWARE
chef's knife, wooden spoon, small bowl, thin metal spatula, large plate, plastic wrap, serrated knife

PREPARATION TIME
30 minutes

DO-AHEAD
The roulades can be made 1 day ahead, covered, and refrigerated overnight. Bring them to room temperature before serving to enhance the flavors.

⅓ cup blue cheese, at room temperature
1 tablespoon heavy cream
Two 12-inch tortilla wraps
6 thin slices prosciutto
3 teaspoons honey mustard
6 large arugula leaves
1 recipe Dried Fig Jam (recipe follows)
Garnish: 1 large bunch arugula, washed, tough stems removed

1. Using a wooden spoon, mix the blue cheese with the cream in the small bowl.

2. Lay the tortillas on a wooden board or work surface. Spread a thin layer of the cheese mixture over two-thirds of each tortilla.

3. Arrange 3 slices of prosciutto horizontally over the cheese on each tortilla. Spread ½ teaspoon of mustard over each slice of prosciutto with the spatula. Arrange 3 arugula leaves lengthwise over the mustard on each tortilla.

4. Roll the tortillas tightly and place them, seam side down, on the plate. Cover the tortillas with plastic wrap and refrigerate for 2 hours or overnight.

5. With a serrated knife, cut the cold tortillas into 12 half-inch-wide diagonal pieces. Turn the individual roulades onto a work surface, filling side up. Place a dollop of Dried Fig Jam in the center of each tortilla with a spoon or pastry bag.

SERVICE   Arrange the roulades on a colorful hors d'oeuvre tray with the arugula bouquet in the center.

COOK'S TIPS   Let the roulades sit at room temperature for 30 minutes before serving to enhance all the flavors inside the wrap. Watercress can be substituted for the arugula.

Dried Fig Jam

KITCHENWARE
chef's knife, medium skillet,
wooden spoon, food processor

PREPARATION
TIME
10 minutes

COOKING TIME
10 minutes

DO-AHEAD
Make the fig jam in advance
and store it, covered, in the
refrigerator for up to 2 weeks.

2 tablespoons extra virgin olive oil
2 medium shallots, finely chopped
½ cup roughly chopped dried figs
¼ cup balsamic vinegar
½ cup port wine
¼ cup red wine

1. Heat the oil over medium heat in the skillet. Add the shallots and sauté until they are translucent and soft, about 3 minutes. Add the figs and continue to sauté, stirring occasionally with a wooden spoon, until the figs have softened, about 3 minutes.

2. Add the vinegar, port, and red wine. Simmer the mixture over medium-high heat until the liquid has reduced and thickened, about 5 minutes. Remove the jam from the heat and cool 10 minutes.

3. With a wooden spoon, transfer the jam to the bowl of the food processor fitted with the steel blade and pulse until the jam reaches a slightly rough consistency. Do not purée the jam.

SERVICE   Use the Dried Fig Jam to top the Prosciutto Tortilla Roulades.

COOK'S TIP   Create a delicious snack by blending 4 ounces of cream cheese with the jam and spreading it on raisin bread.

Portobello Steak Fries with Balsamic—Roasted Garlic Aioli Sauce

KITCHENWARE
chef's knife, aluminum foil–lined baking sheet, 2 medium bowls, wooden spoon, whisk, large skillet, deep-fat thermometer, slotted spoon or metal tongs, paper towel–lined baking sheet

PREPARATION TIME
20 minutes

COOKING TIME
30 minutes

3 portobello mushrooms, washed, dried, and stems removed and discarded
3 large eggs, beaten
$\frac{1}{4}$ cup all-purpose flour
$1\frac{1}{2}$ cups panko crumbs (see Note)
$1\frac{1}{2}$ teaspoons salt
$\frac{1}{4}$ teaspoon cayenne
1 cup vegetable oil
1 recipe Balsamic–Roasted Garlic Aioli Sauce (recipe follows)

1. Slice each portobello cap lengthwise into $\frac{1}{4}$-inch-thick pieces and place them on the aluminum foil–covered baking sheet.

2. Whisk together the eggs and flour in a bowl. With a wooden spoon, blend the panko crumbs, salt, and cayenne together in the other medium bowl.

3. Dip the mushroom slices into the egg batter, then toss them in the seasoned crumbs until well coated.

4. Heat the vegetable oil in the skillet over medium heat until it reaches 375 degrees. Fry the coated mushrooms in batches until they are golden brown, 2 to 4 minutes.

Remove them with a slotted spoon or tongs and place on the paper towel–lined baking sheet to drain.

SERVICE The steak fries look smashing standing up in a tall cylinder-like basket about 8 inches high and 4 inches wide, lined with a white napkin. Guests love dunking the mushrooms in the Balsamic–Roasted Garlic Aioli Sauce.

COOK'S TIP This method of breading is also perfect for bell peppers, shrimp, and scallops.

Note: Panko crumbs are Japanese bread crumbs, available in Asian food markets.

Balsamic—Roasted Garlic Aioli Sauce

KITCHENWARE
pepper mill, food processor,
rubber spatula

PREPARATION
TIME
5 minutes

COOKING TIME
See Roast Garlic (page 286)

DO-AHEAD
The aioli sauce can be made
early in the day and stored,
covered, in the refrigerator.

2 large roasted cloves garlic (see page 286)
1 tablespoon balsamic vinegar
1 teaspoon capers, drained
1 teaspoon Dijon mustard
2 cups mayonnaise
Freshly ground pepper to taste

Put all the ingredients in the bowl of the food processor fitted with the steel blade and process until the sauce is smooth, about 45 seconds. Stop several times to scrape down the sides of the bowl with a rubber spatula. Continue processing until smooth.

SERVICE Serve the sauce in a bowl for dunking the Portobello Steak Fries.

COOK'S TIPS For a chunkier sauce, blend all the ingredients together in a small bowl with a wooden spoon. This sauce is a showstopper as a dip for crunchy vegetable crudités.

Salt-Cured Cilantro-Rubbed Salmon on Cilantro Crostini with Balsamic—Roasted Garlic Aioli Sauce

KITCHENWARE

chef's knife, small bowl, shallow glass baking dish, plastic wrap or aluminum foil, sharp knife

PREPARATION TIME

20 minutes

MARINATING TIME

36 hours

DO-AHEAD

The salmon should be prepared 36 hours before serving.

3 tablespoons kosher or sea salt

2 tablespoons superfine sugar

1 tablespoon minced white Spanish onion

½ teaspoon chili powder

2 teaspoons coarsely ground white pepper

One 10-ounce center-cut salmon fillet

1 small bunch fresh cilantro, coarsely chopped with stems

1 recipe Cilantro Crostini (recipe follows)

1 recipe Balsamic–Roasted Garlic Aioli Sauce (page 34)

Garnish: 1 bunch fresh cilantro, long stems removed

1. Mix together the salt, sugar, onion, chili powder, and white pepper in the small bowl. Rub the mixture into the flesh of the salmon and cover the top with the cilantro.

2. Place the salmon, skin side down, in the baking dish. Cover with plastic wrap or aluminum foil and place a weight (such as a 1-pound can) on top of the salmon.

3. Refrigerate the salmon for 36 hours. Every 8 hours, turn the fish and baste it with the liquid that has accumulated in the bottom of the dish.

4. After the salmon is marinated, drain the liquid and scrape off the coating. Transfer the salmon to a board and cut it into wafer-thin slices on a 45-degree angle with a very sharp knife.

SERVICE Arrange the salmon in overlapping slices on a serving tray. Garnish it with the cilantro and serve it with the Cilantro Crostini and the Balsamic–Roasted Garlic Aioli Sauce.

Cilantro Crostini

KITCHENWARE
chef's knife, bread knife,
food processor, baking sheet,
pastry brush

PREPARATION TIME
10 minutes

COOKING TIME
5 to 7 minutes

DO-AHEAD
Prepare the butter up to 3
days in advance and store it,
covered, in the refrigerator.

2 cups loosely packed fresh cilantro, coarsely chopped
1 medium shallot, coarsely chopped
$\frac{1}{4}$ teaspoon salt
8 tablespoons (1 stick) unsalted butter, at room temperature
One 24-inch slender baguette, sliced on the diagonal into
$\frac{1}{4}$-inch-thick pieces

1. Preheat the oven to 400 degrees.

2. Place the cilantro, shallot, and salt in the bowl of the food processor fitted with the steel blade. Process until smooth. Add the softened butter and process until the mixture is creamy.

3. Place the baguette slices in a single layer on the baking sheet. Generously brush both sides of each piece with the cilantro butter. Bake the crostini, turning them once, 2$\frac{1}{2}$ to 3 minutes per side, until lightly golden and crisp.

SERVICE Pile the crostini into a napkin-lined basket and serve them with the Salt-Cured Cilantro-Rubbed Salmon.

CHAPTER 2

Spring Menus

Snapper with a Mexican Touch

A Chicken Dinner with Asparagus & Rhubarb

Baked Ham Brunch

Two Spring Risottos

A Late-Night Vegetarian Supper

Crisply fried tortillas filled with red snapper,
garlic, chile pepper, and radish scream "South of the Border." Adding
Guacamole and Sour Cream Cilantro Salsas is like topping your
favorite dessert with ice cream and whipped cream. Use a colorful
scarf to decorate the buffet table or dining room table and,
for a fun touch, string up a piñata.
What could be a better addition to the menu than rice cooked in a
saffron-scented broth to create a musky flavor and brilliant yellow color?
Add heat from the chile and the pungent flavor of garlic and you have a
taste-tingling experience. The juicy tang of the grapefruit and lemon acts as a
perfect foil to the heat of the chiles. These fruits, combined with the radicchio
and watercress, are light and complement the rest of the menu.

Snapper with a Mexican Touch

MENU

HORS D'OEUVRE
SUGGESTION
Green Gazpacho Shots (page 20)

RED SNAPPER TOSTADAS WITH
GUACAMOLE AND SOUR CREAM
CILANTRO SALSAS

GOLDEN RICE WITH CHILES

RUBY GRAPEFRUIT SALAD WITH
RADICCHIO AND WATERCRESS

DESSERT SUGGESTION
Chocolate Chocolate Chip Banana
Ice Cream Cake with Pecan Rum Caramel Sauce (page 257)

WINE SUGGESTION:
WHITE
Pinot Grigio, Sauvignon Blanc

Red Snapper Tostadas with Guacamole and Sour Cream Cilantro Salsas

KITCHENWARE
chef's knife, medium saucepan, colander, platter, large stainless-steel or glass bowl, wooden spoons, medium skillet, deep-fat thermometer, slotted spoon, paper towel–lined baking pan

PREPARATION TIME
25 minutes

COOKING TIME
30 minutes

DO-AHEAD
Prepare the onion, garlic, and chile pepper the day before and store them separately, covered, in the refrigerator.

1 bunch fresh cilantro, washed

6 black peppercorns

3 whole cloves

2 tablespoons kosher or sea salt

1 ½ pounds red snapper fillets (see Note)

2 medium white onions, finely chopped

1 large clove garlic, finely chopped

1 serrano or jalapeño chile, seeded and finely minced

3 large tomatoes, coarsely chopped

4 radishes, trimmed and finely diced

Juice of 2 medium limes

1 cup peanut oil

Twelve 6-inch corn tortillas

Table salt and freshly ground pepper

1 cup sour cream

Garnish: 4 bunches fresh cilantro, trimmed, washed, and dried

1 recipe Guacamole Salsa (recipe follows)

1 recipe Sour Cream Cilantro Salsa (recipe follows)

1. Bring 4 cups of water to a boil in the saucepan over high heat with the cilantro, peppercorns, cloves, and kosher or sea salt. Lower the heat to medium and simmer, partially covered, for 10 minutes.

2. Add the snapper and poach the fish 3 to 4 minutes, until it begins to flake when tested with the tines of a fork. Drain the fish in the colander, discarding the liquid. Transfer the fish to the platter and cool in the refrigerator for 5 minutes.

3. While the fish is cooling, combine the onions, garlic, chile, tomatoes, radishes, and lime juice in the large bowl. Flake the snapper into medium pieces and blend it gently with the vegetables using two wooden spoons. Cover the bowl and return it to the refrigerator.

4. Heat the peanut oil in the skillet over medium-high heat until the temperature reaches 330 degrees. Slide the tortillas, one at a time, into the oil and fry 2 to 3 minutes, until golden brown. Transfer them with a slotted spoon to the baking pan.

5. Remove the fish mixture from the refrigerator and season it with table salt and black pepper to taste. Spread 1 tablespoon of sour cream over each warm tortilla. Divide the fish mixture evenly over the sour cream.

SERVICE   Line two large flat baskets with the cilantro. Arrange the tostadas over the leaves. Pass the Guacamole and Sour Cream Cilantro Salsas separately.

COOK'S TIP   For a great munchy, fill a basket with taco chips and serve them with the Guacamole and Sour Cream Cilantro Salsas.

Note: Grouper or halibut is a good substitute for the red snapper.

Golden Rice with Chiles

KITCHENWARE

chef's knife, medium saucepan, medium skillet

PREPARATION TIME

15 minutes

COOKING TIME

20 minutes

DO-AHEAD

Prepare the onion, chile, and garlic the day before. Store them separately, covered, in the refrigerator.

3 ½ cups chicken broth, homemade or low-sodium canned

¾ teaspoon saffron threads

2 tablespoons extra virgin olive oil

1 medium red onion, finely chopped

1 poblano chile, seeded and minced

2 large cloves garlic, finely chopped

1 ½ cups basmati or long-grain white rice, rinsed well (see Note)

½ teaspoon ground chipotle

Salt

Garnish: 2 teaspoons finely chopped fresh flat-leaf parsley

1. Bring the chicken broth to a boil over high heat in the saucepan. Add the saffron threads, stir well, and turn off the heat. Cover the pan and steep the saffron like tea leaves for 15 minutes.

2. While the broth is steeping, heat the oil in the skillet over medium heat. Add the onion and sauté for 3 to 4 minutes. Add the chile and sauté 4 minutes more. Add the garlic and cook for 1 minute. Add the rice and mix; then add the chipotle powder. Cook, stirring often, until the rice is translucent, about 2 minutes.

3. Reheat the broth over high heat. Add the rice mixture and cook it, covered, over medium-low heat until all the

broth has been absorbed, 10 to 12 minutes. Season the rice with salt to taste, blending it well and fluffing the rice. Let stand for 5 minutes off the heat.

SERVICE   Spoon the rice into an earthenware dish. Sprinkle the top with the flat-leaf parsley.

COOK'S TIP   Turn the rice into an entrée by adding 3 large tomatoes, peeled, seeded, and diced, and ¾ pound sautéed diced chorizo sausage, cut into ¼-inch pieces. Substitute cilantro as the garnish for an extra burst of flavor.

Note: Rinse the rice in cold water three or four times, until the water is clear. This will make the rice fluffier.

Ruby Grapefruit Salad with Radicchio and Watercress

KITCHENWARE
pepper mill, chef's knife, small bowl, whisk

PREPARATION TIME
15 minutes

3 ruby grapefruit
2 medium heads radicchio or red leaf lettuce, cored
  and separated into leaves
1 large bunch watercress, washed
2 tablespoons fresh lemon juice
1 teaspoon balsamic vinegar
$\frac{1}{2}$ teaspoon sugar
$\frac{1}{2}$ teaspoon salt
$\frac{1}{4}$ teaspoon freshly ground pepper
$\frac{1}{3}$ cup extra virgin olive oil
$\frac{1}{2}$ cup large pecan pieces

1. Peel and section the grapefruit, carefully removing the white pith. *(The pith tastes bitter.)*

2. Tear the lettuce leaves into 2-inch pieces if they are large. Remove and discard the tough stems of the watercress.

3. Combine the lemon juice, vinegar, sugar, salt, and pepper in the bowl. Whisk the oil into the vinegar mixture and stir until it is well blended.

SERVICE Arrange the radicchio or lettuce leaves in a salad bowl or on a large flat platter. Toss the grapefruit segments with half of the dressing and arrange them in concentric circles over the salad. Place the watercress leaves at random over the grapefruit, sprinkle with the pecans, and pour the remaining dressing evenly over the salad.

COOK'S TIPS Orange sections and alfalfa sprouts can be substituted for the grapefruit and watercress. Peel, seed, and dice 2 avocados for an excellent addition to the salad. For an extra Mexican kick, add 1 tablespoon of chopped fresh cilantro to the dressing.

When you think of roast chicken,
you imagine a bird with crisp, golden skin and moist, succulent meat.
Covering the chicken with a foil tent guarantees a juicy bird. Removing the tent
when the chicken is almost done will turn the skin a rich golden brown.
The citrus glaze enhances the process. The cinnamon and ginger in
the couscous filling act as a fine contrast to the citrus glaze
and permeate the chicken as it roasts.
Rhubarb and strawberries not only are harbingers of spring but also make
a tangy chutney for the roast chicken. It is impossible to resist rhubarb once it
appears in the market. Think of using the chutney as a spread for
biscuits when you want an afternoon snack.
Asparagus, like rhubarb and strawberries, says spring. Though asparagus
is available in our markets all year round, the spring crop is always special
and well priced. Brilliant orange carrots contrasted with the red paprika
in the butter and topped with green chives add
unbelievable color to the menu.

A Chicken Dinner with Asparagus and Rhubarb

MENU

HORS D'OEUVRE SUGGESTION
Prosciutto Tortilla Roulades with Dried Fig Jam (page 29)

**CITRUS-GLAZED ROASTED CHICKEN WITH
GINGER COUSCOUS STUFFING**

**RHUBARB AND
STRAWBERRY CHUTNEY**

ASPARAGUS WITH RED ONION

**ROASTED CARROTS
WITH PAPRIKA BUTTER**

DESSERT SUGGESTION
Creamy Cheesecake with Orange and Chocolate (page 264)

WINE SUGGESTION: WHITE
Pouilly-Fumé, Sancerre

Ginger Couscous Stuffing

KITCHENWARE
chef's knife, grater, medium saucepan, small skillet

PREPARATION TIME
15 minutes

COOKING TIME
35 minutes

DO-AHEAD
Chop the onion, apricots, parsley, and ginger 1 day in advance and store separately, covered, in the refrigerator. Complete entire recipe ahead of time if using for stuffing.

3½ cups chicken broth, homemade or low-sodium canned
½ teaspoon ground cinnamon
½ teaspoon ground ginger
1 pound couscous
5 tablespoons vegetable oil
1 medium onion, finely chopped
1 teaspoon peeled and finely grated fresh ginger
2 tablespoons finely chopped fresh curly parsley
¾ cup dried apricots, finely chopped
1½ teaspoons salt
½ teaspoon freshly ground pepper

1. Bring 2½ cups of the chicken broth to a boil over high heat in the saucepan. Turn off the heat, add the cinnamon and ground ginger, and stir well. Cover and let the broth steep for 15 minutes. Bring the broth back to a simmer and stir in the couscous. Cover and let it stand off the heat for 15 minutes, until the couscous has absorbed the stock. Add more stock as necessary until the couscous is tender but still crunchy.

2. While the couscous is absorbing the broth, heat 2 tablespoons of the oil in the skillet over medium heat. Add the onion and sauté until it is soft, 3 to 4 minutes. Add the fresh ginger and sauté 1 minute. Add the remaining 3 tablespoons oil, the parsley, apricots, and onion to the couscous. Fluff the grains with a fork, mixing and blending all the ingredients. Season with the salt and pepper.

SERVICE After stuffing the chicken, place any leftover couscous in an ovenproof serving dish and bake it, covered, at 350 degrees for about 20 minutes, until heated through.

COOK'S TIP Serve the couscous with roast lamb or pork. The cinnamon, ginger, and apricots are perfect piquant complements for these roasted meats.

Rhubarb and Strawberry Chutney

KITCHENWARE
zester, chef's knife, paring
knife, peeler, medium saucepan

**PREPARATION
TIME**
15 minutes

COOKING TIME
20 minutes

DO-AHEAD
The chutney can be prepared
the day before and stored,
covered, in the refrigerator.
Bring it to room temperature
before serving.

1½ pounds rhubarb, greens removed
Zest and juice of 2 large oranges
½ cup granulated sugar
½ cup packed light brown sugar
2 teaspoons minced ginger
½ cup golden raisins
1 pint strawberries, stemmed and halved

1. Trim the ends of the rhubarb. Scrape the stalks with a peeler if they are dark green and have blemishes. *(It is not necessary to peel the stalks if they are young and bright red.)*

2. Cut the rhubarb into 1-inch pieces and place them in the saucepan with the orange zest and juice, granulated and brown sugars, ginger, and raisins. Simmer uncovered over medium heat, stirring occasionally, until the rhubarb has softened but remains in soft chunks, 15 to 18 minutes.

3. Stir the strawberries into the rhubarb and continue to simmer until the strawberries have just begun to soften but still retain their shape, about 3 minutes more.

4. Cool the chutney to room temperature before serving.

SERVICE Spoon the chutney into a medium bowl to pass around the table when the chicken is served.

COOK'S TIP Serve with roasted, grilled, or broiled meat, chicken, or fish. The flavors in roast beef or roast turkey are enhanced by the chutney served chilled, as a side dish.

Asparagus with Red Onion

KITCHENWARE

chef's knife, zester, large skillet, small skillet, colander

PREPARATION
TIME

5 minutes

COOKING TIME

10 minutes

DO-AHEAD

The asparagus and seasoned olive oil can be prepared 1 day ahead, covered, and refrigerated separately.

2 pounds medium asparagus spears
2 tablespoons extra virgin olive oil
1 medium red onion, finely chopped
Zest and juice of 1 large lemon
Salt and freshly ground pepper
Garnish: 2 teaspoons finely chopped fresh curly parsley

1. Snap off and discard the tough ends of the asparagus. Place the spears in a single layer on a work surface. Trim the asparagus ends so that all the spears are the same length.

2. Place the asparagus in the large skillet and add water to cover. Simmer uncovered over medium heat for 3 to 5 minutes, until they are bright green and crisp to the bite. Drain and shock them in cold water to retain their brilliant green color and texture. Set them aside at room temperature.

3. While the asparagus are cooking, heat the oil in the small skillet over medium heat. Sauté the onion until it is translucent, about 4 minutes. Stir in the lemon zest and juice, blending well, and cool to room temperature.

4. Toss the drained asparagus in the onion mixture for 1 minute. Season with salt and pepper to taste.

SERVICE Arrange the asparagus on a flat serving platter and sprinkle with the chopped parsley.

COOK'S TIP If preparing the recipe in advance, bring the asparagus and seasoned oil back to room temperature before tossing together. Reseason the oil mixture if it has been refrigerated. Garnish with the parsley just before serving.

Roasted Carrots with Paprika Butter

KITCHENWARE
chef's knife, peeler, roasting pan or baking sheet, medium skillet

PREPARATION
TIME
10 minutes

COOKING TIME
30 minutes

DO-AHEAD
The paprika butter may be made up to 2 days ahead, covered tightly, and refrigerated.

1 ½ pounds long, thin carrots, trimmed and peeled, cut into 1 ½-inch-long × ¼-inch-wide sticks
3 tablespoons extra virgin olive oil
½ teaspoon salt
¼ teaspoon freshly ground pepper
5 tablespoons unsalted butter
1 medium onion, finely chopped
2 teaspoons sweet Hungarian paprika
Garnish: 1 teaspoon finely chopped fresh chives

1. Preheat the oven to 350 degrees.

2. Place the carrots in the roasting pan and toss them with the oil, salt, and pepper. Roast the carrots, uncovered, 25 to 30 minutes, until they are tender.

3. While the carrots are roasting, heat 2 tablespoons of the butter over medium heat in the skillet. Sauté the onion until it begins to color, about 5 minutes. Lower the heat and add the remaining butter and the paprika, stirring well until the butter melts, about 1 minute. Toss the roasted carrots with the paprika butter and reseason them with salt and pepper to taste.

SERVICE Serve the carrots piping hot, garnished with the chives.

COOK'S TIP Replace the 2 teaspoons of sweet paprika with ½ teaspoon hot Hungarian paprika to give the carrots a lively bite.

Apricot Mustard–Glazed Smoked Ham

makes a majestic and aromatic centerpiece for a spring brunch.

Yes, the leftovers are serious because the ham is big.

Future meals created with the "extras" will be savored

long after the brunch is over.

Pineapple and ham seem to go together like bacon and eggs. Add the

wonderful flavor of peach to the mix and create a mellow, sweet chutney.

In the salad, the crisp, distinct flavor of licorice in the fennel contrasts

with the tang of the fresh orange to add another taste

dimension to the menu.

Surprise your guests with French toast—not the kind served with maple

syrup, but French toast stuffed with cream and asparagus. Surrounded

by fresh fruit and a green salad, it will

delight your brunch guests.

And about those ham leftovers—remember they are in the freezer

just waiting to be used in the luscious, stick-to-your ribs

Ham and Barley Soup or for a Smoked Ham Hash that, with a poached

egg on top, makes a complete brunch.

Baked Ham Brunch

MENU

HORS D'OEUVRE SUGGESTION
Portobello Steak Fries with Balsamic–Roasted
Garlic Aioli Sauce (page 32)

APRICOT MUSTARD–GLAZED SMOKED HAM

PINEAPPLE PEACH CHUTNEY

FENNEL AND ORANGE SALAD

FRENCH TOAST STUFFED WITH ASPARAGUS
CREAM TOPPED WITH ROASTED RED BELL PEPPER–
BLOODY MARY SAUCE

SERIOUS LEFTOVERS #1: HAM AND BARLEY SOUP

SERIOUS LEFTOVERS #2: SMOKED HAM HASH

DESSERT SUGGESTION
Citrus Pound Cake with Brandied Raisins (page 262)

WINE SUGGESTION: RED
Beaujolais-Villages, Côtes du Rhône

Apricot Mustard— Glazed Smoked Ham

KITCHENWARE

chef's knife, large roasting pan, small saucepan, pastry brush, wooden toothpicks

PREPARATION TIME

5 minutes for glaze

COOKING TIME

2 to 2½ hours

One 6- to 8-pound fully cooked boneless smoked ham

30 to 40 whole cloves

¾ cup apricot preserves

2 tablespoons Dijon honey mustard

¾ cup apple cider

¾ cup apricot nectar

1. Preheat the oven to 325 degrees.

2. Trim off any excess fat from the top side of the ham, leaving a ¼-inch layer of fat. Score the top of the ham in a 1-inch diamond pattern. Spear the center of each diamond with a whole clove. Place the ham in the roasting pan on the center rack of the oven and roast for 1 hour 30 minutes to 1 hour 50 minutes (about 14 minutes per pound).

3. Place the apricot preserves, mustard, cider, and apricot nectar in the saucepan and stir over medium heat until the glaze is reduced and coats the back of a spoon, about 5 minutes. Set aside at room temperature.

4. When the ham is finished, increase the oven temperature to 425 degrees. Rewarm the apricot glaze and brush it generously over the top of the ham. Return the ham to the oven and bake for 20 to 25 minutes, until the glaze has set and caramelized.

SERVICE Slice the ham and arrange it on a serving platter.

COOK'S TIP Carve the leftover ham into ½-inch-thick slices and freeze it in ½-pound packages.

Pineapple Peach Chutney

KITCHENWARE
chef's knife, large skillet or
medium saucepan

**PREPARATION
TIME**
20 minutes

COOKING TIME
20 minutes plus 30 minutes
standing time

DO-AHEAD
Prepare the chutney up to 3
days ahead and store it,
covered, in the refrigerator.

2 tablespoons unsalted butter

2 medium shallots, cut into medium dice

1 teaspoon finely chopped ginger

½ cup dried peaches, cut into medium dice

1 tablespoon balsamic vinegar

1 medium fresh pineapple, trimmed, peeled, cored, and cut into medium dice

¼ cup packed light brown sugar

½ cup peach nectar

1 tablespoon finely chopped fresh mint

1. Heat the butter in the skillet over medium heat and sauté the shallots until they are limp and light golden in color, 5 minutes.

2. Add the ginger, peaches, and vinegar, and simmer for 2 minutes. Add the pineapple, sugar, and peach nectar, and simmer over medium heat until the juices have evaporated, about 15 minutes.

3. Blend the mint into the chutney and simmer 1 minute more. Let the chutney stand at room temperature at least 30 minutes before serving.

SERVICE Serve the chutney at room temperature with the Apricot-Mustard Glazed Smoked Ham.

COOK'S TIP The marriage of this chutney with chicken, roast pork, or lamb results in a wonderful zesty taste.

Fennel and Orange Salad

KITCHENWARE

chef's knife; pepper mill; small, medium, and large bowls; whisk

PREPARATION TIME

25 minutes

1 tablespoon fresh lemon juice
1 tablespoon tarragon vinegar
$\frac{1}{2}$ teaspoon salt
$\frac{1}{4}$ teaspoon freshly ground pepper
6 tablespoons extra virgin olive oil
3 large fennel bulbs
2 tablespoons finely chopped fresh flat-leaf parsley
3 navel or Valencia oranges
Garnish: $\frac{1}{4}$ teaspoon fennel seeds
6 sprigs fennel leaves

1. Combine the lemon juice, vinegar, salt, and pepper in the small bowl. Whisk in the oil and set aside.

2. Trim the leaves from the fennel, reserving 6 sprigs for the garnish. Cut the fennel bulbs in half lengthwise, slice each half into quarters, and remove the core. Cut the fennel into paper-thin slices and place them in the large bowl. Dress the fennel with 2 tablespoons of the vinaigrette, toss it with the parsley, and set aside.

3. Peel the oranges, removing both the membranes and the white pith. Cut the oranges crosswise into very thin rounds. Place them in the medium bowl and dress them with 2 tablespoons of the vinaigrette. Set aside.

SERVICE Layer half the fennel in the bottom of a medium salad bowl. *(The white of the fennel dotted with parsley and the orange of the fruits looks incredible in a glass bowl.)* Arrange half of the orange slices over the fennel in concentric circles. Layer the remaining fennel over the oranges, and arrange the remaining oranges over the fennel. Garnish the salad with the fennel seeds and sprigs and drizzle the remaining vinaigrette over the top.

COOK'S TIP Bunches of watercress or arugula make a fine bed for this salad if you want to introduce a bit more green.

French Toast Stuffed with Asparagus Cream Topped with Roasted Red Bell Pepper—Bloody Mary Sauce

KITCHENWARE

sharp knife, 2 medium bowls, pepper mill, 2 baking dishes large enough to hold all the bread in a single layer, large nonstick skillet, whisk

PREPARATION TIME

25 minutes

COOKING TIME

15 to 20 minutes

DO-AHEAD

Complete the recipe through Step 5 a day in advance of serving.

Six 1½-inch-thick slices day-old challah, brioche, or Italian bread

24 pencil-thin asparagus spears, cooked al dente, cut into ¼-inch dice

4 ounces cream cheese, at room temperature

3 ounces chèvre cheese, at room temperature

2 tablespoons sour cream

1 tablespoon minced scallion

1 teaspoon finely minced fresh rosemary

½ teaspoon salt

¼ teaspoon freshly ground pepper

6 large eggs, beaten

¾ cup heavy cream

3 tablespoons unsalted butter

1 recipe Roasted Red Bell Pepper–Bloody Mary Sauce (recipe follows)

1. Preheat the oven to 375 degrees. Lightly grease one baking dish.

2. Using a sharp knife, cut a horizontal pocket partway through the crust and center of each slice of bread allowing a ¾-inch connection between the halves of each slice.

3. Combine the asparagus, cream cheese, chèvre, sour cream, scallion, and rosemary in a bowl, blending into a cream. Season the mixture with the salt and pepper.

4. Spoon the filling into the bread pockets. Do not overstuff the slices.

5. Whisk the eggs and heavy cream together in the other bowl. Arrange the bread in the ungreased baking dish and pour the custard over it. Soak the slices, turning them once, until they absorb all of the liquid, about 10 minutes. *(The bread can be covered tightly with foil at this point and placed in the refrigerator overnight.)*

6. Melt the butter in the skillet over low to medium heat and sauté the bread, in batches if necessary, until golden, 2 to 3 minutes on each side. Do not overcrowd the skillet. Transfer the toast to the greased baking dish as it is done.

7. Bake until the filling is hot, 8 to 10 minutes.

SERVICE Arrange these golden stuffed pieces of French toast on a platter and pass the Roasted Red Bell Pepper–Bloody Mary Sauce separately.

Roasted Red Bell Pepper—Bloody Mary Sauce

KITCHENWARE

chef's knife, zester, baking sheet, plastic or paper bag, paper toweling, medium saucepan, food processor, pepper mill

PREPARATION TIME

10 minutes

COOKING TIME

15 minutes

DO-AHEAD

The sauce can be made a day in advance, covered, and refrigerated. Bring it to room temperature before serving.

2 large red bell peppers

2 tablespoons extra virgin olive oil

1 medium red onion, finely chopped

1 ½ cups tomato juice

1 teaspoon drained bottled white horseradish

¼ cup vodka

Zest and juice of 1 medium lemon

Salt and freshly ground pepper

1. Preheat the broiler.

2. Place the bell peppers on the baking sheet and set on the rack closest to the broiler unit. Broil the peppers for 6 to 8 minutes, turning them as necessary, until the skins are puffed and blackened on all sides.

3. Remove the bell peppers from the broiler, place them in a bag, and seal the bag immediately. Allow the peppers to steam for 10 minutes. When they are cool enough to handle, slip off the skins and remove the stems and seeds. Rinse the bell peppers, pat dry, and set aside on paper toweling.

4. While the bell peppers cool, heat the oil in the saucepan over medium heat and sauté the onion until it is translucent, 3 to 4 minutes. Raise the temperature to high, add

the tomato juice, and simmer until the juice has reduced by half, about 3 minutes.

5. Transfer the bell peppers, tomato juice, and onion to the bowl of the food processor fitted with the steel blade. Process until the sauce is smooth. Add the horseradish, vodka, lemon zest, and juice, and pulse three times to incorporate the ingredients. Season the sauce with salt and pepper to taste.

SERVICE Put this smoky-flavored, radiantly colored sauce in a deep serving dish and pass it with the French Toast Stuffed with Asparagus Cream.

COOK'S TIPS Grilled vegetables, broiled fish, chicken, and enchiladas are just some of the foods that are perfect to serve with Roasted Red Pepper–Bloody Mary Sauce. Substitute yellow bell peppers for the red, or make two separate recipes using 2 red and 2 yellow bell peppers. Serve both sauces for a stunning presentation.

Serious Leftovers No. 1: Ham and Barley Soup

KITCHENWARE
chef's knife, vegetable peeler,
food processor, large saucepan

PREPARATION TIME
20 minutes

COOKING TIME
50 minutes

DO-AHEAD
Prepare the vegetables up to 1 day ahead, cover, and store them separately in the refrigerator.

1 large white onion, coarsely chopped

2 large carrots, trimmed, peeled, and coarsely chopped

2 celery ribs, trimmed and coarsely chopped

2 parsnips, trimmed, peeled, and coarsely chopped

4 tablespoons ($\frac{1}{2}$ stick) unsalted butter

1 cup pearl barley

2 ham hocks

3 cups chicken broth, homemade or low-sodium canned

2 bay leaves

6 fresh sprigs thyme

6 fresh sprigs flat-leaf parsley

$\frac{3}{4}$ pound ham, cut into $\frac{1}{2}$-inch cubes (left over from the Apricot-Mustard Glazed Smoked Ham)

Garnish: 1 tablespoon finely chopped fresh flat-leaf parsley

1. Put the onion, carrots, celery, and parsnips in the bowl of the food processor fitted with the steel blade and process in batches until finely chopped.

2. Heat the butter in the saucepan over medium heat. Add the vegetables and cook until they begin to soften, 6 to 7 minutes. Add the barley and cook until it begins to soften, stirring often, about 4 minutes more.

3. Add the ham hocks, chicken broth, bay leaves, and thyme and parsley sprigs. Raise the heat to high, bring the liquid to a boil, and remove the scum that forms on the top of the soup. Lower the heat to medium and simmer the soup, partially covered, until the barley has blossomed and is soft, about 40 minutes. Remove and discard the bay leaves, thyme, and parsley.

4. Trim and reserve the meat clinging to the ham hocks. Add these trimmings with the cubed ham to the saucepan and continue to cook for 3 minutes.

SERVICE Serve the soup in deep bowls garnished with the chopped parsley.

COOK'S TIP Adding a green salad and a warm loaf of hearty bread turns this soup into a satisfying meal.

Serious Ham Leftovers No. 2: Smoked Ham Hash

2 pounds Red Bliss potatoes, washed and cut into $\frac{1}{2}$-inch cubes

1 teaspoon plus pinch of salt

$\frac{1}{4}$ cup corn or canola oil

1 medium onion, finely chopped

2 medium cloves garlic, minced

$\frac{1}{2}$ pound domestic mushrooms, washed, dried, and chopped medium

1 medium red bell pepper, cored, seeded, and chopped medium

2 teaspoons finely chopped fresh thyme

$\frac{3}{4}$ pound ham, cut into medium dice (left over from the Apricot Mustard–Glazed Smoked Ham)

$\frac{3}{4}$ cup chicken broth, homemade or low-sodium canned

$\frac{1}{2}$ teaspoon freshly ground pepper

Garnish: 1 tablespoon finely chopped fresh flat-leaf parsley

1. Put the potatoes in the saucepan with water to cover and a pinch of salt. Bring to a boil over high heat and simmer uncovered until the potatoes are fork tender, 15 to 20 minutes. Drain the potatoes and set aside.

2. Heat 2 tablespoons of the oil over medium heat in the skillet. Sauté the onion for 5 minutes, then add the garlic, and cook 1 minute more. Add the mushrooms and red

bell pepper and continue to cook, stirring occasionally, until the vegetables have softened, about 5 minutes more. Blend the thyme, ham, and chicken broth into the vegetables and simmer over medium heat for 4 minutes. Season the mixture with $\frac{1}{2}$ teaspoon of the salt and $\frac{1}{4}$ teaspoon of the pepper and transfer the hash to the bowl.

3. Preheat the oven to 300 degrees.

4. Wipe out the skillet with paper toweling and heat the remaining 2 tablespoons oil over medium-high heat. Add the drained potatoes and cook until they are lightly browned, 5 to 6 minutes. Stir the potatoes and continue to cook until they are browned on all sides, about 4 minutes more.

5. Add the vegetables and ham mixture to the potatoes and cook the hash over medium heat until it is heated through. Season it again with the remaining $\frac{1}{2}$ teaspoon salt and $\frac{1}{4}$ teaspoon pepper.

6. Transfer to the casserole and keep it warm in the oven until ready to serve.

SERVICE Just before serving, garnish the top of the casserole with the chopped parsley.

COOK'S TIPS Leftover chicken, beef, lamb, and certainly corned beef, the traditional hash partner, can be substituted for the ham. Top it with poached eggs for a Sunday brunch.

Create an unusual spring Italian menu
with not one, but two risottos: one with shrimp and
wild mushrooms, the other with sun-dried
tomatoes, zucchini, and eggplant.
Place the casseroles of rice next to each other so your
guests can appreciate the brilliant colors of the saffron risotto
and the bright pink shrimp contrasted with the deep red and
green of the sun-dried tomatoes and freshly chopped basil.
The hint of salt in the anchovies, married with broccoli and bell peppers,
brings spice and color to the menu. The slight bite of the arugula and the
lemon zest in the focaccia complete the perfect picture.
Serve this menu informally and let your guests help themselves
to a relaxing celebration of spring.

MENU

HORS D'OEUVRE
SUGGESTION
Honey-Glazed Chicken Wings (page 25)

SAFFRON RISOTTO WITH
SHRIMP AND WILD MUSHROOMS

RISOTTO WITH SUN-DRIED TOMATOES,
ZUCCHINI, AND EGGPLANT

BROCCOLI WITH BELL PEPPERS
AND ANCHOVIES

ARUGULA AND LEMON
TAPENADE FOCACCIA

DESSERT SUGGESTION
Peach Yogurt Tea Cake (page 271)

WINE SUGGESTION: WHITE
Sauvignon Blanc, Pinot Blanc

Saffron Risotto with Shrimp and Wild Mushrooms

KITCHENWARE

chef's knife, grater, medium saucepan, large Dutch oven, 2 medium bowls

PREPARATION TIME

30 minutes

COOKING TIME

40 minutes

DO-AHEAD

Prepare the onion, garlic, and parsley and grate the cheese the day before. Store them separately, covered, in the refrigerator.

6 cups chicken broth, homemade or low-sodium canned

1 teaspoon saffron threads

3 tablespoons extra virgin olive oil

¾ pound shiitake or porcini mushrooms, wiped clean with dry paper toweling or brushed clean, cut into ½-inch-thick slices

1 teaspoon salt

½ teaspoon ground white pepper

1 pound medium shrimp, peeled and deveined

1 teaspoon fresh lemon juice

2 tablespoons unsalted butter

1 medium onion, finely chopped

2 medium cloves garlic, finely minced

2 cups short-grain rice, such as Arborio or Carnaroli

¼ cup dry white wine

½ cup freshly grated Parmesan cheese

2 teaspoons finely chopped fresh flat-leaf parsley

1. Bring the chicken broth to a boil over high heat in the saucepan. Add the saffron, stir well, and turn the heat to low. Simmer uncovered for 10 minutes.

2. Heat 2 tablespoons of the oil in the Dutch oven over high heat. Add the mushrooms and season them with ¼ tea-

spoon of the salt and ⅛ teaspoon of the pepper; sauté until they are lightly browned, about 5 minutes. Remove the mushrooms to a bowl.

3. Heat the remaining 1 tablespoon of oil in the same pan over high heat. Add the shrimp and sauté with ¼ teaspoon salt and ⅛ teaspoon pepper until the shrimp just turn pink, about 1 minute. Sprinkle the lemon juice over the shrimp and set them aside in a bowl.

4. Reduce the heat to medium-low and add the butter to the pan. Add the onion, season it with the remaining ½ teaspoon salt and ¼ teaspoon pepper, and cook until soft and translucent, 5 to 8 minutes. Add the garlic and cook 1 minute more.

5. Add the rice and stir to coat the grains with the butter and onion. Cook until the rice turns opaque, 3 to 5 minutes. Add the wine and simmer until it evaporates.

6. Add ½ cup of the simmering broth to the rice and, stirring frequently, simmer until almost all of the broth is absorbed. Continue adding broth in ½-cup increments, stirring frequently and adjusting the heat as necessary to maintain a simmer.

7. After all of the broth has been used, add the mushrooms and check the rice for doneness. It should be soft to the bite but not mushy. If necessary, add ½ cup of hot water.

8. When the rice is done, add the reserved shrimp, the Parmesan, and the parsley. Correct the seasoning if necessary and serve.

SERVICE Spoon the piping hot risotto into deep soup bowls. Pass extra Parmesan cheese on the side and have a pepper mill on the table. For buffet service, place the risotto in a deep casserole.

COOK'S TIP Substitute ½ pound fresh lump crabmeat for the shrimp in Step 8, eliminating Step 3.

Risotto with Sun-Dried Tomatoes, Zucchini, and Eggplant

KITCHENWARE

chef's knife, grater, medium saucepan, large Dutch oven, large bowl

PREPARATION TIME

30 minutes

COOKING TIME

40 minutes

DO-AHEAD

Prepare the zucchini, onion, and garlic the day before and store them separately, covered, in the refrigerator.

6 cups beef broth, homemade or low-sodium canned

$\frac{1}{4}$ cup extra virgin olive oil

2 Japanese eggplants (about 8 ounces each), trimmed, cut into small dice

1 teaspoon salt

$\frac{1}{2}$ teaspoon freshly ground pepper

2 medium zucchini (about 8 ounces each), cut into small dice

4 tablespoons finely chopped drained oil-packed sun-dried tomatoes

1 medium red onion, finely chopped

2 cloves garlic, minced

2 cups short-grain rice, such as Arborio or Carnaroli

$\frac{1}{4}$ cup dry white wine

$\frac{1}{2}$ cup freshly grated pecorino cheese

3 tablespoons finely chopped fresh basil

1. Heat the beef broth to a gentle simmer in the saucepan.

2. Heat 2 tablespoons of the oil in the Dutch oven over medium heat. Add the eggplants, season them with $\frac{1}{4}$ teaspoon of the salt and $\frac{1}{8}$ teaspoon of the pepper, and sauté until lightly browned, 3 to 5 minutes. Add the zucchini, season with $\frac{1}{4}$ teaspoon of the salt and $\frac{1}{8}$

teaspoon of the pepper, and cook for 2 to 3 minutes. Add the tomatoes, cook for 1 minute, remove the vegetables to the bowl and reserve.

3. Return the pan to medium-low heat, and add the remaining 2 tablespoons oil and the onion. Season with the remaining $\frac{1}{2}$ teaspoon salt and $\frac{1}{4}$ teaspoon pepper, and sauté until translucent and tender, 5 to 8 minutes. Add the garlic and cook 1 minute more.

4. Add the rice, and stir to coat the grains with the onion and oil. Cook until the rice turns opaque, 3 to 5 minutes. Add the wine and simmer until it evaporates.

5. Add $\frac{1}{2}$ cup of the simmering broth to the rice and, stirring frequently, simmer until almost all the broth is absorbed. Continue adding broth in $\frac{1}{2}$-cup increments, stirring frequently and adjusting the heat as necessary to maintain a simmer.

6. After all the broth has been used, add the reserved vegetables and check the rice for doneness. The risotto should be creamy and the rice should be soft but not mushy. If necessary, add $\frac{1}{2}$ cup of hot water.

7. Add the pecorino and basil, correct the seasoning, and serve immediately.

SERVICE Spoon the piping hot risotto into deep soup bowls. Pass extra pecorino cheese and have a pepper mill on the table. For buffet service, place the risotto in a deep casserole.

Broccoli with Bell Peppers and Anchovies

KITCHENWARE

chef's knife, small bowl, pepper mill, medium saucepan, colander, salad bowl

PREPARATION TIME

20 minutes

MARINATING TIME

30 minutes

COOKING TIME

1½ to 2 minutes

DO-AHEAD

The bell peppers and broccoli can be prepared early in the day and refrigerated separately. Toss the ingredients together and finish the recipe no more than 30 minutes before serving.

1 large clove garlic, finely chopped

4 tablespoons extra virgin olive oil

1 tablespoon balsamic vinegar

1 tablespoon finely chopped fresh parsley

1 tablespoon finely chopped fresh oregano

2 tablespoons finely chopped fresh chives

2 yellow bell peppers, cored, seeded, and cut lengthwise into ¼-inch-wide strips

1½ teaspoons salt

¼ teaspoon freshly ground pepper

3½ pounds broccoli, cut into small florets

6 anchovy fillets in oil, drained and cut into small pieces

½ cup pine nuts

1. Combine the garlic, olive oil, vinegar, parsley, oregano, and chives in the small bowl. Mix the bell pepper strips with the marinade, blending well. Season the mixture with ½ teaspoon of the salt and the pepper. Set aside at room temperature or refrigerate until 30 minutes before serving.

2. While the bell peppers are marinating, bring 3 quarts of water and the remaining 1 teaspoon salt to a boil in the saucepan over high heat. Add the broccoli, lower the heat to medium, and simmer uncovered for 1½ to 2 minutes. Immediately drain the broccoli well in the colander and

shock it in cold water; drain. *(The broccoli will be very crisp.)* Place it in the salad bowl or refrigerate it until 30 minutes before serving.

SERVICE Toss the broccoli with the marinated bell peppers, the anchovy fillets, and the pine nuts. Reseason with salt and pepper. Serve the salad within 30 minutes. The marinated broccoli will lose its vibrant green color if it rests too long in the marinade.

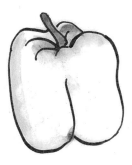

Arugula and Lemon Tapenade Focaccia

KITCHENWARE

zester, pastry brush, 9 x 12-inch baking pan, 2 small bowls, 2 large bowls, wooden spoon, plastic wrap, food processor, kitchen towel, rack

PREPARATION TIME

45 minutes plus 2 hours rising time

COOKING TIME

40 to 45 minutes

FOCACCIA DOUGH

8 tablespoons ($\frac{1}{2}$ cup) extra virgin olive oil
1 package active dry yeast
2$\frac{3}{4}$ to 3 cups all-purpose flour
1 teaspoon salt

ARUGULA TAPENADE TOPPING

1$\frac{1}{4}$ cups pitted kalamata or niçoise olives
$\frac{3}{4}$ cup pitted cracked green olives
4 cloves garlic
$\frac{1}{2}$ cup (4 ounces) oil-packed tuna fish, drained
2 tablespoons drained capers
$\frac{1}{3}$ cup extra virgin olive oil
Zest of 1 lemon
8 ounces arugula leaves, washed and chopped
Garnish:1 small bunch arugula

1. Brush the baking pan with 2 tablespoons of the olive oil and set it aside.

2. **Make the focaccia dough:** Place 1 cup warm water in a small bowl, sprinkle the yeast over the water, and set aside for 3 minutes, until the yeast dissolves. Add 4 tablespoons of the olive oil.

3. Using a wooden spoon, stir together 2$\frac{3}{4}$ cups of the flour, the salt, and the yeast mixture in a large bowl. Work the

dough until it comes together into a ball. Place the dough on a lightly floured work surface and knead it until the dough is soft but somewhat sticky, about 3 minutes. Add the ¼ cup of remaining flour as necessary to facilitate kneading the dough. Shape the dough into a ball. Grease the other large bowl with 1 tablespoon of the oil, add the dough, cover the bowl with plastic wrap, and let rise in a warm place for 1 ¼ hours.

4. **Make the topping:** While the dough is rising, place the black and green olives in the bowl of the food processor fitted with the steel blade, and purée until smooth. Add the garlic, tuna, capers, and ⅓ cup oil, and pulse until the tapenade is puréed. Transfer to a small bowl. Blend the lemon zest into the mixture and set it aside.

5. Punch down the dough with your hands and press it into the prepared baking pan, covering the entire surface. Brush the dough with the remaining 1 tablespoon of oil. Let the dough rise again for 45 minutes, covered with a kitchen towel or plastic wrap.

6. While the dough is rising, preheat the oven to 400 degrees.

7. With your fingers, make ½-inch indentations all over the top of the dough, about 1 ½ inches apart. Spread the tapenade over the dough, using all of the mixture.

8. Bake the focaccia for 40 to 45 minutes, until the crust is golden. Immediately transfer the focaccia to a rack until it has cooled. Distribute the fresh arugula leaves over the focaccia, slice it into 2 ½ × 2-inch pieces, and serve at room temperature.

SERVICE Line a flat basket with a large decorative napkin. Arrange the focaccia pieces over the napkin. Place small bunches of arugula on each end of the basket.

COOK'S TIPS Spread a layer of tomato sauce over the focaccia dough before spreading it with the tapenade. Sprinkle a few grinds of black pepper over the tapenade, then add the arugula. For a thinner focaccia, use a larger (12 × 17-inch) baking pan.

After a visit to an art gallery or attending a great show,
your hungry guests will be thrilled with this late-evening dinner of
rich Spinach-Laced Moussaka. Serve this meal right from the kitchen.
Moussaka has always shouted richness and needs a crisp,
cooling partner. The Asparagus Slaw does that for this menu.
No discussion here of preferring soft or
hard asparagus—this elegant vegetable must be presented *crisp*.
Because there can never be too many beans on a vegetarian menu,
smash them and serve them on crisp toast for a perfect accompaniment.
Deep ruby red beets roasted with nutty caraway butter add the
finishing touch, taste, and color.
Serve a Pinot Noir and give your guests the chance to
relax after an evening of entertainment.

A Late-Night Vegetarian Supper

MENU

HORS D'OEUVRE SUGGESTION
Miniature Eggplant Crisps (page 27)

SPINACH-LACED MOUSSAKA

ASPARAGUS SLAW

SMASHED WHITE BEAN MASH
ON TOASTED BREAD

ROASTED BEETS WITH
CARAWAY BUTTER

DESSERT SUGGESTION
Chocolate Chocolate Chip Walnut Brownies (page 260)

WINE SUGGESTION: RED
Pinot Noir

Spinach-Laced Moussaka

KITCHENWARE

chef's knife, grater, 2 baking
sheets, large skillet, pepper
mill, paper toweling, pastry
brush, small saucepan, whisk,
medium rectangular or oval
oven-to-table casserole

PREPARATION
TIME

60 minutes

COOKING TIME

30 minutes

DO-AHEAD

Moussaka is best when
prepared the day before. Finish
the recipe through Step 6
without baking. Cover the dish
and refrigerate. Bring the
moussaka to room
temperature and bake as
directed.

2 medium eggplants (about 2 pounds total), cut into
$\frac{1}{4}$-inch-thick rounds

1 $\frac{1}{2}$ teaspoons salt

5 tablespoons extra virgin olive oil

1 large Spanish onion, finely chopped

3 medium cloves garlic, finely chopped

1 $\frac{1}{2}$ pounds wild mushrooms (shiitake, oyster, or cremini),
washed and dried, or wiped and brushed, finely chopped

1 tablespoon tomato paste

One 14-ounce can plum tomatoes, drained

$\frac{1}{2}$ cup red wine

1 tablespoon finely chopped fresh oregano

$\frac{1}{4}$ teaspoon ground cinnamon

1 teaspoon freshly ground pepper

$\frac{1}{2}$ cup half-and-half

4 ounces cream cheese, at room temperature

One 10-ounce package frozen chopped spinach, defrosted
and squeezed dry (see Note)

$\frac{1}{4}$ teaspoon ground allspice

1 cup coarsely grated Asiago cheese

2 tablespoons medium grated pecorino cheese

1. Arrange the eggplant rounds on a baking sheet. To extract
the water from the eggplant, sprinkle it lightly with $\frac{1}{2}$
teaspoon of the salt and set it aside for about 30 minutes.

2. Heat 2 tablespoons of the oil in the skillet
and sauté the onion over medium heat until

soft, about 3 minutes. Add the garlic and cook 1 minute more. Add the mushrooms and cook, stirring occasionally, until they have softened and released their juices, 5 to 6 minutes. Blend the tomato paste, tomatoes, wine, oregano, and cinnamon into the mixture. Season the sauce with $\frac{1}{2}$ teaspoon of the salt and $\frac{1}{2}$ teaspoon of the pepper, and simmer it on low heat, uncovered, for 10 minutes, until it has a paste-like consistency.

3. Preheat the broiler. While the sauce simmers, pat the eggplant dry with paper toweling. Brush both sides of each round lightly with the remaining oil, and broil the eggplant 6 inches from the heat until golden brown, 5 to 6 minutes. *Watch carefully.* Remove it from the broiler and set it aside.

4. Preheat the oven to 400 degrees. Lightly grease the casserole.

5. In a small saucepan, combine the half-and-half and cream cheese. Warm the mixture over low heat, stirring it with a whisk, until blended, 2 to 3 minutes. Mix in the spinach and season the mixture with the remaining salt and pepper and the allspice.

6. Layer half the eggplant, browned side up, in the prepared casserole. Cover it with a layer of the mushroom mixture, and sprinkle it with half the Asiago. Repeat the process with the remaining eggplant and mushroom mixture. Spoon the spinach cream sauce over the mushrooms and sprinkle the top with the remaining Asiago and the pecorino. Bake uncovered 25 to 30 minutes, until the top is golden brown.

SERVICE Bring the piping-hot moussaka to the table and serve it from the casserole, or let your guests help themselves to this rich, bubbly entrée.

COOK'S TIP Sautéed zucchini or yellow squash can be layered in the baking dish with the eggplant.

Note: Defrost spinach in a microwave and squeeze out the excess liquid with a clean kitchen towel.

Asparagus Slaw

KITCHENWARE

chef's knife, grater, salad bowl, small bowl, small whisk, pepper mill

PREPARATION TIME

30 minutes

DO-AHEAD

Prepare all the vegetables early in the day and store them separately, covered, in the refrigerator.

THE SLAW

1 bunch (about 1 pound) medium asparagus spears, cut on the diagonal into $\frac{1}{2}$-inch pieces

4 large radishes, trimmed and finely chopped

2 medium carrots, peeled and coarsely grated

2 large celery ribs, trimmed and cut crosswise into thin slices

1 yellow bell pepper, cored, seeded, and cut into medium dice

3 scallions, washed, trimmed, and cut into $\frac{1}{4}$-inch-thick slices

THE DRESSING

1 tablespoon fresh lemon juice

1 tablespoon sherry vinegar

1 tablespoon honey

$\frac{1}{2}$ teaspoon Dijon mustard

$\frac{1}{3}$ cup vegetable oil

1 teaspoon finely chopped fresh flat-leaf parsley

1 teaspoon finely chopped fresh tarragon

2 teaspoons mustard seeds

$\frac{1}{2}$ teaspoon salt

$\frac{1}{4}$ teaspoon freshly ground pepper

1. Make the slaw: Toss the asparagus, radishes, carrots, celery, bell pepper, and scallions together in the salad bowl.

2. Make the dressing: Blend the lemon juice, vinegar, honey, and mustard together in the small bowl. Slowly whisk the oil into the vinegar mixture, blending well. Season the dressing with the parsley, tarragon, mustard seed, salt, and pepper.

SERVICE Pour the vinaigrette over the Asparagus Slaw 30 minutes before serving. Season it again with salt and pepper to taste.

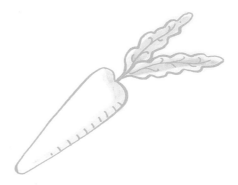

Smashed White Bean Mash on Toasted Bread

KITCHENWARE

chef's knife, grater, food processor, small bowl, wooden spoon, pepper mill, serrated knife, pastry brush, baking sheet

PREPARATION TIME

15 minutes

COOKING TIME

8 minutes for toast

See Roast Garlic (page 286).

DO-AHEAD

Prepare the bean mash 1 day ahead and add parsley just before serving. The toasted bread can be completed 2 days before serving. Line a plastic container with paper toweling and fill it with the toasted bread. Cover it well with an airtight lid and store it in a cool place at room temperature.

WHITE BEAN MASH

One 19-ounce can cannellini beans, drained well
6 medium roasted cloves garlic (see page 286)
¼ cup drained oil-packed sun-dried tomatoes
2 tablespoons extra virgin olive oil
¼ cup sour cream
1 teaspoon fresh lemon juice
1 tablespoon finely chopped fresh flat-leaf parsley
Salt and freshly ground pepper

TOASTED BREAD

1 medium loaf French, Italian, or peasant bread, 2½ to
    3 inches in diameter
2 tablespoons extra virgin olive oil
¾ cup finely grated Parmesan cheese
Garnish: 2 teaspoons finely chopped fresh flat-leaf parsley
2 cups niçoise olives

1. **Make the mash:** Place the beans in the bowl of the food processor fitted with the steel blade and pulse until they are puréed. Add the garlic and sun-dried tomatoes and pulse twice, just until the tomatoes have blended with the bean purée.

2. Slowly pour the oil into the beans through the feeding tube, pulsing the machine. Transfer the mash to the small bowl and, with a wooden spoon, thoroughly blend in the sour cream, lemon juice, and parsley. Season the mixture with salt and pepper to taste.

3. **Toast the bread:** Preheat the broiler.

4. Cut the bread into $\frac{1}{2}$-inch-thick slices with a serrated knife. Brush both sides of each bread round with the oil.

5. Place the rounds on the ungreased baking sheet and toast them under the broiler about 5 inches from the heating element for 4 to 5 minutes, until they are golden brown.

6. Cover the untoasted side of the rounds with the Parmesan and return to the broiler for 4 to 5 minutes, until the cheese is bubbly and golden brown.

SERVICE Spoon the mash into a soup crock or a medium bowl and sprinkle it with the parsley. Place the olives in a small bowl next to the mash. Arrange the toasted bread in a cloth napkin–lined shallow bread basket. Slathering the mash on the toasted bread is a labor of love for your guests.

COOK'S TIPS If you made the mash and toast in advance, bring the beans to room temperature and gently rewarm the toast in the oven before serving. If you like a little heat, add $\frac{1}{2}$ teaspoon Tabasco sauce to the mash.

Roasted Beets with Caraway Butter

3 pounds small beets (weighed without greens), washed and trimmed

2 tablespoons extra virgin olive oil

4 tablespoons (½ stick) unsalted butter

3 tablespoons honey

½ teaspoon Dijon mustard

Zest and juice of 1 medium lemon

1 teaspoon caraway seeds

Garnish: ½ teaspoon finely chopped fresh flat-leaf parsley

1. Preheat the oven to 350 degrees.

2. Toss the beets in the bowl with the oil, transfer them to the baking sheet, and roast in the oven 35 to 40 minutes, until fork tender. *(Large beets may take 1¼ hours to roast.)*

3. While the beets are roasting, heat the butter in the saucepan over medium heat. Stir in the honey and cook, stirring, until it has dissolved. Add the mustard, lemon zest and juice, and caraway seeds; cook over low heat until the mixture thickens, about 3 minutes. Set it aside at room temperature.

4. Remove the beets from the oven and set them aside until they are cool enough to handle, 5 to 7 minutes. Peel the beets with a paring knife or vegetable peeler. (The skins will come off quite easily.) Cut each one into quarters. If using large beets, cut them into eighths.

5. Transfer the beets to the saucepan with the butter mixture. Stir the beets until they are glazed with the honey butter.

SERVICE Spoon the beets and sauce into a white crockery dish and sprinkle with the chopped parsley.

COOK'S TIPS Add ½ cup of walnut pieces to the beets for extra crunch. Substitute orange juice for the lemon juice for added sweetness.

CHAPTER 3

Summer Menus

A Shrimp Feast

Summer Turkey Teriyaki

Pulled-Pork Barbecue

Season's Bounty Pasta Frittata

Vegetarian Supper on the Grill

Just the aroma of these grilled Asian shrimp
will make your guests salivate with anticipation. Light the charcoal fire
and, in no time, you'll be serving this tangy, irresistible entrée.
Red tomatoes, yellow tomatoes, orange tomatoes,
striped tomatoes, beefsteak tomatoes, teardrop tomatoes,
cherry tomatoes—the list goes on and on.
Find the juiciest vine-ripened tomatoes you can, preferably
from your own garden. Any combination of color and size will do.
Use the best extra virgin olive oil available, then top all of this with
fresh basil and cracked black pepper for the consummate summer salad
to serve with the savory shrimp.
A twist on hot potato salad marries broccolini and Red Bliss potatoes.
The green broccolini, the red potatoes, the multicolored tomatoes, and the
bright rosy pink of the shrimp bring an air of festivity to your table.
Then finish the menu with a loaf of bread—not just any bread,
but bread filled with cheese, prosciutto, and arugula. This colorful
barbecue menu just screams "informality."

A Shrimp Feast

MENU

HORS D'OEUVRE SUGGESTION
Gorgonzola and Caramelized Onion Tart (page 16)

**GRILLED ASIAN JUMBO SHRIMP WITH
SPICY MANGO CHUTNEY**

A RAINBOW OF TOMATOES

**CHILE-SPICED BROCCOLINI AND
RED BLISS POTATOES**

**A LOAF OF BREAD, CHEESE,
ARUGULA, AND PROSCIUTTO**

DESSERT SUGGESTION
Peach Yogurt Tea Cake (page 271)

WINE SUGGESTION: WHITE
Pinot Grigio, Pinot Blanc

Grilled Asian Jumbo Shrimp with Spicy Mango Chutney

KITCHENWARE

chef's knife, large stainless-steel or glass bowl, plastic wrap, six 8 to 10-inch wooden skewers, pastry brush, tongs

PREPARATION TIME

30 minutes

MARINATING TIME

30 minutes

COOKING TIME

4 minutes

DO-AHEAD

Prepare the garlic, shallots, and ginger the day before. Cover and store them separately in the refrigerator.

2 large cloves garlic, peeled and finely minced

2 large shallots, peeled and finely minced

1 teaspoon finely minced ginger

2 tablespoons rice wine vinegar

$\frac{1}{4}$ cup oyster sauce

2 tablespoons fresh lime juice

3 tablespoons honey

30 jumbo shrimp (under 15 count; approximately 2 pounds), peeled, deveined, tails removed

Vegetable oil for brushing the grill

2 tablespoons extra virgin olive oil

Garnish: 1 medium head Boston lettuce or other light greens

12 small lemon wedges

1 recipe Spicy Mango Chutney (recipe follows)

1. Combine the garlic, shallots, ginger, vinegar, oyster sauce, lime juice, and honey in the large bowl. Set the mixture aside for 10 minutes. Add the shrimp and toss well to coat each one. Marinate the shrimp for 30 minutes, covered with plastic wrap, in the refrigerator.

2. While the shrimp are marinating, soak the skewers in warm water for 30 minutes.

3. Light a charcoal grill and wait until the coals are gray, or preheat a gas grill. Brush the grill grate with vegetable oil.

4. Thread 5 shrimp on each skewer, piercing them through the center and allowing 1 ½ inches between shrimp. Brush them with any leftover marinade.

5. Lightly brush both sides of the shrimp with the olive oil and place them on the hot grill for about 2 minutes. Turn the shrimp and grill until the centers are opaque, about 2 minutes more. Do not overcook the shrimp or they will become tough and dry.

SERVICE Arrange the skewers on a bed of Boston lettuce leaves in a flat woven basket or on a platter. Place the lemon slices around the skewers. Pass the Spicy Mango Chutney separately.

COOK'S TIP It's fun to have your guests slide the shrimp off the skewers themselves, but the shrimp can also be placed on the platter unskewered, if you prefer.

Spicy Mango Chutney

KITCHENWARE

chef's knife, large skillet, medium bowl

PREPARATION TIME

30 minutes

COOKING TIME

12 minutes

DO-AHEAD

The chutney can be made up to 3 days ahead and stored, covered, in the refrigerator.

2 tablespoons extra virgin olive oil

4 medium shallots, finely chopped

2 large cloves garlic, minced

1 small jalapeño chile, seeded and diced

$\frac{1}{3}$ cup dry white wine

$\frac{1}{4}$ cup fresh orange juice

1 teaspoon ground cumin

1 tablespoon finely chopped fresh flat-leaf parsley

1 tablespoon finely chopped fresh cilantro

2 large ripe mangoes, peeled, pitted, and diced medium

1. Heat the oil in the skillet over medium heat and sauté the shallots for 3 minutes. Add the garlic and jalapeño and continue to sauté the vegetables for 2 minutes more. Stir in the wine, orange juice, cumin, parsley, and cilantro; lower the heat to medium-low and simmer for 5 minutes more.

2. Blend the mangoes into the chutney and simmer for 3 minutes. Transfer the chutney to the bowl, set aside, and cool at room temperature.

SERVICE Serve this colorful and tasty chutney in a glass bowl with the Grilled Asian Jumbo Shrimp.

COOK'S TIP If you like hot chutney, increase the jalapeño or use a hotter pepper, such as a serrano.

A Rainbow of Tomatoes

KITCHENWARE
serrated or sharp slicing knife, large platter, pepper mill

PREPARATION TIME
20 minutes

2 large vine-ripened yellow tomatoes
2 large vine-ripened red tomatoes
2 large vine-ripened orange or peach tomatoes
½ pint red teardrop or grape tomatoes
½ pint yellow teardrop tomatoes
⅓ cup extra virgin olive oil
6 large sprigs fresh basil
Freshly ground pepper to taste

1. Cut the yellow, red, and orange tomatoes into 4 slices each. Arrange in overlapping slices on a large platter, alternating the colors every two slices.

2. Place the yellow and red teardrop tomatoes over the sliced tomatoes.

3. Drizzle the oil over the salad.

SERVICE Arrange the basil sprigs over the tomatoes, grind pepper over the salad, and leave the pepper mill on the table.

COOK'S TIPS Slices of fresh mozzarella or Asiago cheese can be added to the salad. Add anchovy fillets for guests addicted to this salty, piquant fish.

Chile-Spiced Broccolini and Red Bliss Potatoes

KITCHENWARE

chef's knife, grater, large saucepan, colander, large bowl, pepper mill, large skillet

PREPARATION TIME
20 minutes

COOKING TIME
25 minutes

DO-AHEAD
Prepare the potatoes the day before, cover them with water, and store them, covered, in the refrigerator. Also, prepare the onion, garlic, and cheese and store them separately, covered, in the refrigerator. Prepare the broccolini 2 hours before serving.

1 pound medium Red Bliss potatoes, unpeeled, cut into ½-inch-thick wedges

3 teaspoons salt

6 tablespoons extra virgin olive oil

1½ tablespoons red wine vinegar

1 medium red onion, finely chopped

¼ teaspoon freshly ground pepper

¾ pound broccolini

3 medium cloves garlic, finely sliced

½ teaspoon hot red pepper flakes

½ cup pine nuts

½ cup finely grated Parmesan cheese

1. Put the potatoes in the saucepan and add cold water to cover and ½ teaspoon of the salt; bring to a boil over high heat. Lower the heat to medium and simmer the potatoes, uncovered, until they are just fork tender, 8 to 10 minutes. Drain the potatoes, place them in the bowl, and toss them while still hot with 3 tablespoons of the oil, the vinegar, and the onion. Season with ½ teaspoon of the salt and ¼ teaspoon of the black pepper, and set aside at room temperature.

2. While the potatoes are marinating, trim the bottom 1 inch from the broccolini florets. Cut the vegetable into 1-inch pieces. Place water to cover plus 2 teaspoons salt in the saucepan; bring to a boil over high heat. Lower the heat to medium, add the broccolini, and simmer until it is just resistant to the tines of a fork, 4 to 5 minutes. Drain the broccolini in a colander, shock it in cold water, and drain it again.

3. Heat the remaining 3 tablespoons of the oil in the skillet over medium heat and sauté the garlic until it is golden, about 3 minutes. Add the broccolini, red pepper flakes, and pine nuts and sauté for 2 to 3 minutes, stirring often.

4. Drain any remaining marinade from the potatoes.

SERVICE   Gently combine the potatoes and broccolini in a large salad bowl. Season again with salt and black pepper to taste, and sprinkle with the Parmesan.

COOK'S TIP   This salad tastes best when served at room temperature.

A Loaf of Bread, Cheese, Arugula, and Prosciutto

KITCHENWARE
chef's knife, 2 medium bowls, pastry brush, pepper mill, 10 x 15-inch piece aluminum foil, serrated knife

PREPARATION TIME
15 minutes

COOKING TIME
5 to 6 minutes

DO-AHEAD
The recipe can be prepared through Step 5 early in the day, and refrigerated.

4 tablespoons extra virgin olive oil
1 tablespoon finely chopped fresh oregano
1 long loaf Italian or French bread or 2 medium-size loaves, halved lengthwise
1 small bunch arugula, washed
½ teaspoon salt
8 ounces Brie, cut into ¼-inch-thick slices
6 ounces prosciutto, cut paper thin
½ teaspoon freshly ground pepper

1. Preheat the grill, or preheat the oven to 350 degrees.

2. Combine 3 tablespoons of the oil with the oregano in a bowl. Brush both sides of the bread with the oregano-scented oil.

3. Toss the arugula with the remaining 1 tablespoon of oil and the salt in the other bowl, coating all the leaves well.

4. Cover the bottom half of the bread with slices of the Brie. Place the arugula over the Brie and cover it with the prosciutto. Sprinkle the prosciutto with the pepper.

5. Cover the layered bottom half of bread with the top. Place the bread, top side down, on the aluminum foil and crimp the edges of the foil well to seal the bread in the package. Set it aside at room temperature if it is to be used within 1 hour, or refrigerate if preparing it earlier in the day.

6. Place the foil-covered bread on the grill for 4 minutes or in the oven for 8 to 10 minutes.

SERVICE Transfer the bread from the foil to a cutting board. *(Watch your hands—the bread is hot!)* Cut the loaf into 1 ½-inch-thick pieces with a serrated knife and serve it warm from the cutting board.

COOK'S TIP Substitute St. André, Saga blue, or Fontina for the Brie to please the palate with another taste.

What a surprise for your guests
to be dining on turkey "London Broil" instead of the
usual beef! The breast meat of the turkey is succulent
and moist when marinated in a combination of soy sauce,
orange juice, vinegar, and brown sugar. The flavor of the summery
Peach Strawberry Chutney, boosted with ginger and brown sugar, provides
the perfect complement to the turkey.
A hash made with potatoes, apple-smoked bacon,
and crunchy vegetables, tossed with subtle Roasted Shallot
Garlic Oil, rounds out the menu.

Summer Turkey Teriyaki

MENU

HORS D'OEUVRE SUGGESTION
Asian-Spiced Scallop Saté (page 10)

**TERIYAKI TURKEY LONDON BROIL
WITH PEACH STRAWBERRY CHUTNEY**

**GRILLED SUMMER SQUASH
WITH LEMON VINAIGRETTE**

**POTATO HASH WITH ROASTED
SHALLOT GARLIC OIL**

DESSERT SUGGESTION
Blackberry Brandy
Fresh Plum Bread Pudding (page 252)

WINE SUGGESTION: RED
Cabernet Sauvignon, Merlot

Teriyaki Turkey London Broil with Peach Strawberry Chutney

KITCHENWARE
chef's knife, medium saucepan, plastic wrap–lined baking sheet, pastry brush, sharp carving knife

PREPARATION TIME
15 minutes

MARINATING TIME
2 hours or overnight

COOKING TIME
40 minutes

DO-AHEAD
Marinate the turkey.

1 cup Japanese dark soy sauce
½ cup fresh orange juice
¼ cup rice vinegar
3 tablespoons light brown sugar
3 tablespoons finely chopped onion
2 medium cloves garlic, finely minced
2 tablespoons minced ginger
One 6- to 8-pound turkey breast, boned, skinned, and butterflied (see Note)
1 recipe Peach Strawberry Chutney (recipe follows)

1. Combine the soy sauce, orange juice, vinegar, sugar, onion, garlic, and ginger in the saucepan. Heat the marinade over medium-high heat, stirring occasionally, and simmer briskly for 3 minutes. Set it aside and cool for 5 minutes.

2. Place the turkey breast on the baking sheet and brush both sides with ¾ cup of the marinade. Marinate for 2 hours at room temperature or overnight, covered, in the refrigerator. (Store the remaining marinade in the refrigerator as well.)

3. To grill the turkey breast, allow the coals on a charcoal grill to turn gray, or preheat a gas grill to medium or low heat. Bring the turkey breast to room temperature, if refrigerated.

4. Brush the top side of the breast with half the remaining marinade, and grill it for 15 minutes. Turn the breast, brush it well with the remaining marinade, and grill it for an additional 15 minutes. (The internal temperature for the fully cooked turkey breast should be 160 degrees.)

5. Transfer the turkey to a cutting board and carve the meat on the diagonal, against the grain, into $\frac{1}{4}$-inch-thick slices.

SERVICE Ask your guests to step up to the grill and help themselves to turkey, or arrange the slices on a platter. Pass the Peach Strawberry Chutney.

COOK'S TIPS Leftover turkey makes wonderful sandwiches. Slather the Peach Strawberry Chutney on slices of bread and pile on the turkey. To keep the meat moist, make sure to cover the turkey well before refrigerating it.

Note: Ask your butcher to bone, skin, and butterfly the turkey breast. *(Freeze the bones and use them to enrich a soup broth.)*

Peach Strawberry Chutney

KITCHENWARE
chef's knife, paring knife, medium skillet

PREPARATION TIME
20 minutes

COOKING TIME
12 minutes

DO-AHEAD
The chutney can be made up to 3 days ahead and stored, covered, in the refrigerator.

1 tablespoon unsalted butter
2 tablespoons finely chopped onion
1 tablespoon finely chopped ginger
2 tablespoons light brown sugar
$\frac{1}{3}$ cup fresh orange juice
1 tablespoon fresh lemon juice
2 tablespoons cider vinegar
$\frac{1}{4}$ cup dry red wine
3 large ripe but firm peaches, cut into $\frac{1}{2}$-inch pieces
1 pint strawberries, stemmed

1. Melt the butter in the skillet over medium heat. Add the onion and ginger and sauté for 3 minutes. Add the brown sugar, orange juice, lemon juice, vinegar, and wine, and simmer for 3 minutes. Add the peaches and simmer for 3 minutes more.

2. Cut the strawberries in half if they are small, or in quarters if they are large. Stir the strawberries into the peach mixture in the skillet and simmer for 2 minutes. Cool the chutney to room temperature before serving.

SERVICE To take advantage of the vibrant colors of the peaches and strawberries, and add a festive touch, serve the chutney in a glass bowl.

COOK'S TIP Substitute 5 large apricots for the strawberries. Simmer the apricots with the peaches in Step 1 for a Peach Apricot Chutney.

Grilled Summer Squash with Lemon Vinaigrette

KITCHENWARE
chef's knife, pepper mill,
large bowl

**PREPARATION
TIME**
10 minutes

COOKING TIME
10 minutes

6 small young green squash (zucchini), about 4 inches long, trimmed and sliced in half lengthwise
6 small young yellow squash, about 4 inches long, trimmed and sliced in half lengthwise
1 $\frac{1}{2}$ tablespoons extra virgin olive oil
$\frac{1}{2}$ teaspoon salt
$\frac{1}{4}$ teaspoon freshly ground pepper
2 beefsteak tomatoes, cut into $\frac{1}{4}$-inch-thick slices
1 recipe Lemon Vinaigrette (recipe follows)

1. Preheat a charcoal grill until the charcoal turns gray or preheat a gas grill.

2. Toss the green and yellow squash with the oil, salt, and pepper in the bowl.

3. Grill the squash, skin side down, about 6 inches from the coals, until it is a light golden brown, about 5 minutes. Turn the squash and grill the other side for 3 to 5 minutes more.

SERVICE Cover a large platter with overlapping slices of tomatoes. Arrange the squash, skin side down, over the tomatoes, alternating the green and yellow colors. About $\frac{1}{2}$ hour before serving, dress the squash with the Lemon Vinaigrette. The pungent flavors of the vinaigrette are at their peak when this dish is served at room temperature.

COOK'S TIP To make the recipe indoors, heat 2 tablespoons of olive oil in a large skillet over medium-high heat. Sauté the squash halves, in batches, skin side up, until the bottoms are golden brown, 2 to 3 minutes. Turn the squash and sauté the skin side for 2 minutes more, adding more olive oil as needed. Season the squash with salt and pepper and transfer it to a baking pan lined with paper toweling. Proceed with the service as written.

Lemon Vinaigrette

1 large clove garlic, coarsely chopped

½ cup fresh basil

½ teaspoon Dijon mustard

1 tablespoon balsamic vinegar

Zest and juice of 1 lemon

⅓ cup extra virgin olive oil

1 teaspoon salt

½ teaspoon freshly ground pepper

1. Place the garlic, basil, mustard, vinegar, and lemon zest and juice in the bowl of the food processor fitted with the steel blade. Process the mixture until it is puréed.

2. With the motor running, slowly pour the oil through the feed tube, until the dressing has thickened. Season it with the salt and pepper.

SERVICE Drizzle the vinaigrette over the Grilled Summer Squash.

Potato Hash with Roasted Shallot Garlic Oil

KITCHENWARE

chef's knife, large skillet, paper towel–lined baking sheet, medium saucepan, colander, slotted spoon, pepper mill

PREPARATION TIME

30 minutes

COOKING TIME

35 minutes

DO-AHEAD

Prepare the hash early in the day and store it, covered, in the refrigerator. Bring it to room temperature and reseason before serving.

½ pound apple-smoked bacon, cut into ¼-inch dice

1 teaspoon kosher salt

1 pound Red Bliss potatoes, unpeeled, cut into ½-inch dice

1 pound peas in the pod (about 1 cup shelled)

½ pound baby green beans, trimmed and cut into thirds

1 large red onion, finely chopped

2 red bell peppers, cored, seeded, and finely chopped

2 cups corn kernels (about 4 ears)

4 scallions, thinly sliced

3 tablespoons finely chopped fresh flat-leaf parsley

1 teaspoon table salt

½ teaspoon freshly ground pepper

3 tablespoons Roasted Shallot Garlic Oil (recipe follows)

1. Sauté the bacon in the skillet until crisp. Transfer it to the baking sheet. Reserve the rendered fat in the pan.

2. Bring 8 cups of water and the kosher salt to a boil over high heat in the saucepan. Add the potatoes and boil for 5 minutes, then remove them to the colander with a slotted spoon. *The potatoes should be crisp to the bite.* Rinse or shock the potatoes with cold water, then drain when cool.

3. In the same water, repeat this procedure with the shelled peas, cooking them for 3 minutes. Repeat the procedure with the green beans, cooking them for 4 to 5 minutes.

4. Heat the reserved bacon fat in the skillet over medium heat and sauté the onion until it is translucent, 3 to 4 minutes. Add the bell pepper and continue to sauté the vegetables until they have softened but are still crisp, about 4 minutes. Add the potatoes and sauté another 10 minutes, until crisp. Add the corn, peas, and beans, and sauté another 5 minutes.

5. Combine the scallions, parsley, and bacon with the vegetables and season the mixture with table salt and pepper. Dress the hash with the Roasted Shallot Garlic Oil.

SERVICE Serve the vegetable hash as a room-temperature salad or heat it in a 350-degree oven for about 20 minutes and serve warm.

COOK'S TIPS Diced sautéed pancetta or regular bacon can be substituted for the apple-smoked bacon. Feel free to substitute other vegetables, such as asparagus, carrots, or baby artichokes. Remember to adjust the cooking times so that the vegetables are crisp to the bite when prepared: asparagus, 3 to 4 minutes; carrots, 4 to 6 minutes; and baby artichokes, 10 to 12 minutes.

Roasted Shallot Garlic Oil

KITCHENWARE

paper toweling, chef's knife, small casserole or 12 x 18-inch piece of aluminum foil, slotted spoon, food processor

PREPARATION TIME

10 minutes

COOKING TIME

45 minutes

DO-AHEAD

The Shallot Garlic Oil can be made up to 1 week ahead and stored, covered, in the refrigerator.

4 large shallots

2 large heads garlic

2 tablespoons plus 2 cups extra virgin olive oil

½ teaspoon salt

1. Preheat the oven to 350 degrees.

2. Wash the skins of the shallots and the garlic heads to remove any dirt. Dry them well with paper toweling. Cut off the root end of each vegetable.

3. Place the vegetables in the casserole and drizzle them with 2 tablespoons of the oil, or place them on the aluminum foil, drizzle them with the oil, and seal the foil tightly.

4. Roast the shallots and garlic, covered, for 45 to 50 minutes. Remove them from the oven and transfer them with a slotted spoon onto paper toweling to drain. When the vegetables are cool enough to handle, place the garlic bulbs and shallots on a cutting board and press the pulp out with the heel of your hand.

5. Transfer the shallot and garlic pulp to the bowl of a food processor fitted with the steel blade. Add 1 cup of the oil and process until the purée begins to blend with the oil.

Add the remaining 1 cup oil and the salt and process for 1 minute more. Remove the Shallot Garlic Oil to a glass container and store it, covered, for up to 1 week in the refrigerator.

COOK'S TIP   The oil adds incredible and piquant flavor to beef, lamb, or poultry when brushed on the meat 30 minutes before broiling or grilling.

Create a pure homespun menu and let your guests "pull"
the pork. Read through the easy recipe to see what pulling is all about.
Cover the pork with Spicy Barbecue Sauce and heap it all onto a
curry-spiced buttered hamburger roll.
The perfect accompaniment, Down-Home Baked Beans, covered with
molasses, brown sugar, and bourbon, will make your guests beg to be invited
back or at least ask for your recipe. Add the crunchy Jicama and Snow Pea Salad
Dressed in Fresh Peach Vinaigrette for a cooling foil.
This is a sloppy menu, and you'll need lots of napkins and
"moist towelettes" for your guests.

Pulled-Pork Barbecue

MENU

HORS D'OEUVRE SUGGESTION
Garlicky Doused Shrimp (page 13)

**SLOW-COOKED SPICY
PULLED BARBECUED PORK
WITH SPICY BARBECUE SAUCE
ON CURRY-SPICED BUTTERED BUNS**

DOWN-HOME BAKED BEANS

**JICAMA AND SNOW PEA SALAD
DRESSED IN FRESH PEACH VINAIGRETTE**

DESSERT SUGGESTION
Chocolate Chocolate Chip Banana Ice Cream Cake
with Pecan Rum Caramel Sauce (page 257)

WINE SUGGESTION: RED
Cabernet Sauvignon, Merlot

Slow-Cooked Spicy Pulled Barbecued Pork with Spicy Barbecue Sauce on Curry-Spiced Buttered Buns

KITCHENWARE

large glass or stainless steel bowl, plastic wrap, large oven-to-table baking dish with cover, meat thermometer, aluminum foil, basting brush, medium saucepan

PREPARATION TIME

5 minutes

MARINATING TIME

1 day

COOKING TIME

2½ hours

DO-AHEAD

The pork can be braised up to 3 days ahead and stored, covered, in the refrigerator.

2 boneless pork butts, about 2 pounds each
1 recipe Spicy Barbecue Sauce (recipe follows)
1 recipe Curry-Spiced Buttered Buns (recipe follows)

1. Put the pork butts in the bowl and pour half the Spicy Barbecue Sauce over them. Refrigerate the rest of the sauce to serve with the cooked pork. Cover the pork with plastic wrap and marinate in the refrigerator for 1 day, turning it once as it marinates.

2. Choose either braising or grilling method.

BRAISING METHOD

❧ Bring the pork to room temperature 2 hours before braising.

❧ Preheat the oven to 325 degrees.

❧ Place the pork and marinade in the baking dish and braise it, covered, for 2½ hours, or until it is so tender that the meat begins to fall apart when pierced with the tines of a fork. (The interior temperature of the pork should be 160 degrees.) Remove the pork from the sauce.

❧ Bring the pork to room temperature 2 hours before grilling.

❧ Preheat a gas grill to 250 degrees. The pork must be grilled over moderate heat so it does not dry out yet the tissues break down during the cooking process, allowing it to fall apart in tender chunks when pulled. Do not allow the temperature of the grill to rise above 275 degrees.

❧ Grill the pork, covered, for 2½ hours, turning and brushing it with the marinade every 25 minutes. The pork is ready when it falls apart when tested with the tines of a fork.

3. While the pork is cooking, make the Curry-Spiced Buttered Buns. Wrap the buns in aluminum foil and set them aside at room temperature. *(If you are grilling the meat, the buns can be heated over the low-temperature part of the grill just before serving.)*

4. When the meat is cool enough to handle, literally pull it apart with the tines of a fork or with your fingers. The meat will resemble randomly shredded chunks. Place the pork in the baking dish and keep it warm over low heat on top of the stove or in a 250-degree oven. If the pork is not to be served immediately, cool it to room temperature in the baking dish before refrigerating.

SERVICE Heat the reserved barbecue sauce in the saucepan over medium heat. Pour the sauce into a serving bowl. Place the buns in a flat basket. Serve the pulled pork in the baking dish and watch your guests enjoy this earthy meal.

Spicy Barbecue Sauce

KITCHENWARE

chef's knife, zester, large saucepan, pepper mill, wooden spoon, food processor

PREPARATION TIME

30 minutes

COOKING TIME

70 minutes

DO-AHEAD

The entire sauce recipe can be made in advance and stored, covered, in the refrigerator up to 3 days.

¼ cup peanut oil

2 large onions, finely chopped

6 large cloves garlic, finely minced

Four 14-ounce cans whole peeled plum tomatoes with their juice, broken up with a spoon

2 tablespoons tomato paste

2 teaspoons chili powder

½ cup honey

½ teaspoon red pepper flakes

Zest of 2 oranges

1 cup red wine vinegar

Salt and freshly ground pepper

1. Heat the oil in the saucepan over medium heat. Add the onions and sauté them for 4 minutes. Add the garlic and continue to sauté 2 minutes more. With a wooden spoon, blend in the plum tomatoes with their juice, the tomato paste, chili powder, honey, red pepper flakes, orange zest, and vinegar. Bring the sauce to a high simmer, then lower the heat to medium-low and simmer the sauce, uncovered, for 1 hour, stirring occasionally. Season with salt and black pepper to taste.

2. Cool the sauce to room temperature and divide it into two batches. Refrigerate one batch for the marinade. Pour the remaining sauce into the large bowl of the food processor fitted with the steel blade and process until smooth. This batch will be served as the sauce.

COOK'S TIPS This sauce freezes well and is perfect for chicken, lamb, or spare ribs.

Curry-Spiced Buttered Buns

KITCHENWARE
chef's knife, small saucepan,
wooden spoon, pastry brush

PREPARATION TIME
15 minutes

COOKING TIME
10 minutes

DO-AHEAD
The butter can be prepared 3
days in advance, cooled to
room temperature, and
stored, covered, in the
refrigerator.

8 tablespoons (1 stick) unsalted butter, at room temperature
3 tablespoons finely chopped red onion
1 medium clove garlic, finely minced
$\frac{1}{2}$ teaspoon finely minced ginger
$\frac{1}{2}$ teaspoon curry powder
$\frac{1}{4}$ teaspoon salt
12 hamburger buns

1. Heat 2 tablespoons of the butter in the saucepan over medium heat and sauté the onion for 3 minutes, until it is limp and translucent. Add the garlic and continue to sauté for 1 minute.

2. Add the remaining 6 tablespoons butter, the ginger, curry, and salt to the saucepan and blend the ingredients with a wooden spoon. Simmer the butter over medium-low heat for 4 minutes to meld all the seasonings.

SERVICE Brush the buns with the butter mixture.

COOK'S TIP Substitute pita pockets for the hamburger buns.

Down-Home Baked Beans

KITCHENWARE

chef's knife, medium bowl, medium saucepan, colander, medium oven-to-table baking dish with cover, pepper mill, wooden spoon

PREPARATION TIME

20 minutes
plus overnight soaking time

COOKING TIME

2 hours 10 minutes

DO-AHEAD

Soak the beans overnight. This recipe can be completed a day in advance and the beans stored, covered, in the refrigerator. To reheat, see the Cook's Tips.

1 pound dried small white navy beans

1 large yellow onion, finely chopped

2 large cloves garlic, finely chopped

¼ cup dark molasses

1 cup packed dark brown sugar

2 teaspoons dry mustard

2 tablespoons bourbon

½ cup tomato sauce

¼ teaspoon ground cloves

½ teaspoon salt

¼ teaspoon freshly ground pepper

½ pound honey-baked ham, unsliced, from the supermarket delicatessen

1. Pick over the beans, discarding any pebbles. Soak the beans overnight in the bowl with enough water to cover. The next day, rinse the beans and discard the water.

2. Place the beans in the saucepan and cover with cold water. Bring the water to a boil over high heat, reduce the heat to medium, and simmer the beans, uncovered, for 1 hour, until they are tender but remain crisp to the bite.

3. Preheat the oven to 325 degrees.

4. Drain the beans in the colander, reserving the liquid. Place the beans in the baking dish. Add the onion, garlic, molasses, sugar, mustard, bourbon, tomato sauce, cloves,

salt, and pepper, and combine all the ingredients with a wooden spoon. Add 2 cups of the reserved cooking liquid to cover the beans by $\frac{1}{2}$ inch. Stir well, cover, and bake the beans for 40 minutes.

5. While the beans are baking, cut the ham into $\frac{1}{2}$-inch cubes. After 40 minutes, add the ham to the beans and continue to bake, covered, another 30 minutes. Add more cooking liquid if the tops of the beans look dry.

6. Uncover the beans, raise the oven temperature to 400 degrees, and continue to bake another 40 minutes. Once again, if the beans look dry, add more cooking liquid to cover.

SERVICE Serve the beans piping hot, right out of the molasses-encrusted baking dish.

COOK'S TIPS Don't toss out that reserved cooking liquid. Store it, covered, in the refrigerator. If you prepare the beans the day before, bring them to room temperature and reheat them, covered, in a 325-degree oven. The reserved liquid will keep the beans moist while they are reheating.

Jicama and Snow Pea Salad Dressed in Fresh Peach Vinaigrette

KITCHENWARE

chef's knife, medium saucepan, colander, paper toweling or kitchen towel, salad bowl, peeler, food processor, pepper mill

PREPARATION TIME

40 minutes

DO-AHEAD

The snow peas, jicama, and pineapple can be prepared 1 day ahead and stored, covered separately, in the refrigerator.

1 1/2 pounds snow peas, trimmed, strings removed

1 teaspoon salt

1 1/2 pounds jicama

1 medium pineapple, trimmed and peeled

1 medium ripe peach

2 teaspoons fresh lemon juice

1 tablespoon balsamic vinegar

1/2 teaspoon sugar

1/3 cup extra virgin olive oil

Freshly ground pepper

Garnish: 6 sprigs fresh mint

1. Bring 2 quarts of water to a boil in the saucepan over high heat. Drop the peas and 1 teaspoon salt into the water and blanch for 1 minute. Drain the peas in the colander and rinse them for 30 seconds in cold water. Lay the peas over paper toweling or a kitchen towel to dry. Slice them into 1/4-inch julienne strips and place them in a salad bowl.

2. Peel the jicama and slice it into quarters, then cut each quarter into 1/4-inch julienne strips. Toss the jicama with the snow peas.

3. Cut the pineapple lengthwise into 1/4-inch-thick slices. Cut each slice into 1/4-inch julienne strips and toss them with the snow peas and jicama.

4. Bring 1 quart of water to a boil in the saucepan over high heat. Drop the peach into the water, lower the heat to medium, and simmer the peach for 1 minute. Peel the peach, remove the pit, and roughly chop the flesh.

5. In the bowl of the food processor fitted with the steel blade, purée the peach, lemon juice, vinegar, and sugar until smooth. Add the oil and pulse just until the ingredients have blended. Season the vinaigrette with salt and pepper to taste.

SERVICE About ½ hour before serving, gently toss the salad with the peach vinaigrette, using two wooden spoons or salad servers and coating all the ingredients well. Set the mint sprigs over the top of the salad and refrigerate until serving.

Summertime is "tomato time," with an abundance
of classic red ones as well as yellow beefsteaks readily available
in markets. For the soup recipe, buy ripe yellow tomatoes and
serve the soup hot, at room temperature, or chilled. Everyone will be
delighted and ask for seconds.

An irresistible accompaniment to the Yellow Tomato Soup
is the ham and cheese Summer Pasta Frittata, filled with onions, basil,
prosciutto, and mozzarella. The child in your guests will love this
as much as "mac and cheese."

And, as an homage to the abundance of summer fruits, top off the
meal with refreshing, delicious Nectarines and
Plums Poached in Red Wine.

Season's Bounty Pasta Frittata

MENU

HORS D'OEUVRE
SUGGESTION
Grilled Meatballs with Indian-Spiced
Yogurt Sauce (page 22)

YELLOW TOMATO SOUP

SUMMER PASTA FRITTATA

NECTARINES AND
PLUMS POACHED IN RED WINE

ZUCCHINI AND ONION BREAD

ORANGE HONEY BUTTER

DESSERT SUGGESTION
Creamy Cheesecake with
Orange and Chocolate (page 264)

WINE SUGGESTION: RED
Chianti

Yellow Tomato Soup

KITCHENWARE
chef's knife, large saucepan,
food processor, fine-mesh
strainer

PREPARATION
TIME
40 minutes

COOKING TIME
30 minutes

DO-AHEAD
The vegetables can be
chopped 1 day ahead and
stored separately, covered, in
the refrigerator.

3 tablespoons extra virgin olive oil

1 pound leeks, white part only, coarsely chopped

1 pound fennel, white part only, coarsely chopped

1 large Spanish onion, coarsely chopped

2 large cloves garlic, coarsely chopped

½ pound celery, white part only, coarsely chopped

3½ pounds yellow beefsteak tomatoes, quartered

1 quart chicken broth, homemade or low-sodium canned

1 small bay leaf

1 sprig fresh thyme

½ teaspoon kosher salt

¼ teaspoon white pepper

Table salt and freshly ground black pepper

1 tablespoon champagne vinegar

Garnish: 2 tablespoons crème fraîche or sour cream

¼ teaspoon finely chopped fresh thyme

1. Warm the oil over medium-low heat in the saucepan. Add the leeks, fennel, onion, garlic, and celery. Cover the pot and slowly cook the vegetables until they are soft and translucent, about 10 minutes. Do not allow the vegetables to color.

2. Add the tomatoes, raise the heat to medium-high, and sauté the vegetables 5 minutes.

3. Add the chicken broth, bay leaf, thyme, kosher salt, and white pepper and simmer the soup over medium heat for 12 to 15 minutes. The tomatoes will release their flavor and produce a tangy taste.

4. Remove the bay leaf and thyme sprig. Purée the soup in the bowl of the food processor fitted with the steel blade, then strain it through the strainer and season it to taste with table salt and black pepper. The soup should have a smooth body with a medium-thick consistency.

5. Cool the soup until it is just warm and add the vinegar. Adjust the seasonings, if necessary. Serve hot or chilled.

SERVICE Ladle the soup into individual soup bowls and garnish each dish with a dollop of the crème fraîche combined with the chopped thyme.

COOK'S TIP Use only ripe, flavorful tomatoes. Out-of-season tomatoes will not give good results.

Summer Pasta Frittata

KITCHENWARE

chef's knife, grater, large saucepan, colander, wooden spoon, small skillet, 2 large bowls, pepper mill, large nonstick ovenproof skillet

PREPARATION TIME

30 minutes

COOKING TIME

20 to 25 minutes

DO-AHEAD

The pasta can be cooked 1 day in advance and stored, covered, in the refrigerator. Bring the refrigerated pasta to room temperature before completing the recipe.

1 tablespoon plus $\frac{1}{2}$ teaspoon salt

$\frac{1}{2}$ pound uncooked linguine

5 tablespoons extra virgin olive oil

1 medium onion, chopped medium

8 large eggs, beaten

6 ounces prosciutto, thinly sliced and julienned into $\frac{1}{4}$-inch-wide strips

1 $\frac{1}{2}$ cups coarsely grated mozzarella cheese

2 tablespoons finely chopped fresh basil

2 teaspoons finely chopped fresh curly parsley

$\frac{1}{4}$ teaspoon freshly ground pepper

$\frac{1}{2}$ cup freshly grated Parmesan cheese

Garnish: 8 sprigs fresh curly parsley

$\frac{1}{2}$ cup finely grated Parmesan cheese

1. Bring 6 quarts of water and 1 tablespoon of the salt to a rolling boil over high heat in the saucepan. Add the linguine and cook over medium heat until it is al dente, or firm to the bite, 8 to 10 minutes. Drain the pasta through a colander. Run cold water through the pasta, shaking out the excess water. Place the pasta in a large bowl and, using a wooden spoon, toss it with 1 tablespoon of the oil.

2. Heat 2 tablespoons of oil in the skillet. Add the onion and sauté it over medium heat for 3 minutes. Set aside.

3. In a bowl, combine the eggs, prosciutto, mozzarella, onion, basil, parsley the remaining $\frac{1}{2}$ teaspoon salt, the pepper, and the pasta, using two kitchen forks.

4. Preheat the oven to 350 degrees.

5. Coat the bottom and sides of the skillet with the remaining 2 tablespoons of oil. Pour the frittata mixture into the skillet.

6. Cook the frittata over medium-low heat, undisturbed, for 8 to 10 minutes, until the eggs begin to pull away from the sides of the pan and the bottom of the frittata is firm. Sprinkle $\frac{1}{2}$ cup of the Parmesan over the frittata and transfer the skillet to the oven. Bake the frittata until it is set, about 20 minutes. Let the frittata cool for 5 minutes, then slip it out of the skillet onto a large round serving platter.

SERVICE   Cut the frittata into pie-shaped $2\frac{1}{2}$-inch-wide wedges and garnish it with the curly parsley. Put the pepper mill and a small bowl with the remaining Parmesan next to the frittata so guests can help themselves.

COOK'S TIP   Diced bell peppers, quartered thin asparagus spears, sautéed wild mushrooms, sautéed sausage meat, or leftover diced chicken are just some of the fine foods that can be added to the frittata.

Nectarines and Plums Poached in Red Wine

KITCHENWARE
chef's knife, skillet or saucepan
large enough to hold the fruit
in a single layer, slotted spoon

PREPARATION
TIME
15 minutes

COOKING TIME
8 to 10 minutes

DO-AHEAD
The entire recipe can be made
the day before, and the fruit
and glaze refrigerated
separately.

1 cup sugar

2 cups full-bodied red wine, such as Zinfandel or Cabernet

¼ cup fresh orange juice

2 tablespoons fresh lemon juice

1 cinnamon stick

3 whole cloves

6 medium-ripe firm nectarines, halved and pitted

6 medium-ripe firm red plums, halved and pitted

Garnish: 2 tablespoons coarsely chopped, unsalted pistachio nuts

10 sprigs fresh mint

1. Combine the sugar, red wine, orange juice, lemon juice, cinnamon, and cloves in the skillet, and bring the mixture to a boil over high heat.

2. Place the fruit in the poaching liquid, skin side up. Reduce the heat to medium-low and simmer until the fruit is barely tender, 3 to 5 minutes.

3. Using a slotted spoon, remove the fruit and place the halves, skin side up, in concentric circles on a serving platter. If you are not serving the fruit immediately, cover it lightly and refrigerate it.

4. Reduce the poaching liquid over medium heat until it forms a thick syrup, about 5 minutes. Discard the cinnamon stick and cloves.

SERVICE Drizzle the top of the fruit with the syrup. Sprinkle the pistachio nuts over the top of the fruit and garnish it with mint sprigs. The fruit can also be served in individual dishes and garnished the same way.

COOK'S TIP If the entire recipe is made the day before, take the chill off the fruit by bringing it to room temperature for 20 minutes before serving. At the same time, warm the glaze very gently until it is thin enough to drizzle over the fruit.

Zucchini and Onion Bread

KITCHENWARE

chef's knife, food processor, medium skillet, pepper mill, greased large bowl, kitchen towel or plastic wrap, greased 8- or 9-inch round baking pan, pastry brush, rack

PREPARATION TIME

30 minutes plus 1½ hours rising time

COOKING TIME

30 minutes

DO-AHEAD

Prepare the onion and zucchini up to 1 day ahead and store them separately, covered, in the refrigerator.

1 tablespoon active dry yeast

2 tablespoons sugar

¼ teaspoon saffron threads

2 tablespoons extra virgin olive oil

1 medium yellow onion, finely chopped

1 teaspoon salt

¼ teaspoon freshly ground pepper

3 cups zucchini, washed and cut into 2-inch dice

2 teaspoons Dijon mustard

4 to 4½ cups unbleached flour

Egg wash (see page 285)

1. Dissolve the yeast and sugar in ½ cup warm water in the bowl of the food processor. Add the saffron and stir well.

2. Heat the oil over medium heat in the skillet and sauté the onion for 2 to 4 minutes. Season it with ½ teaspoon of the salt and the pepper. Add the zucchini and sauté it for 5 to 8 minutes, stirring occasionally. Remove the vegetables from the skillet and cool to room temperature.

3. Add the zucchini and onion, the remaining ½ teaspoon salt, the mustard, and 4 cups of the flour to the yeast mixture and stir well. Process the dough, using the steel blade, until the mixture leaves the sides of the bowl and begins to form a ball. If the dough is too wet, add a bit more flour until the consistency of the dough is slightly

sticky. *(If you are not using the food processor, knead all the ingredients on a wooden board until the dough is smooth, elastic, and slightly sticky to the touch, adding more flour as necessary, about 10 minutes.)*

4. Place the dough in the greased bowl. Cover the top with a towel or plastic wrap, and set it aside to rise in a warm place for 1 hour.

5. Transfer the dough to a floured surface and knead it a few times. Put the dough in the prepared baking pan, lightly cover with a damp towel or plastic wrap, and allow it to rise for 30 minutes.

6. Preheat the oven to 375 degrees.

7. Brush the top of the dough with the egg wash and bake about 45 minutes, until it is golden brown.

SERVICE Cool the bread for 5 minutes in the pan, then invert it onto a cake rack. Bring the bread to the table on a cutting board with a bread knife and let your guests help themselves. Serve with the Orange Honey Butter.

COOK'S TIPS This recipe can be doubled. Freeze the second loaf for future use. Substitute eggplant or yellow squash for the zucchini. Add 1 minced large clove garlic to the skillet when sautéing the onion to give the bread an extra kick.

Orange Honey Butter

KITCHENWARE
**zester, grater, medium bowl,
wooden spoon**

PREPARATION
TIME
10 minutes

DO-AHEAD
**Make the butter up to 2 days
ahead and store it, covered, in
the refrigerator.**

8 tablespoons (1 stick) unsalted butter, at room temperature
2 tablespoons honey
1 tablespoon orange zest
2 tablespoons fresh orange juice
1 teaspoon grated ginger

1. Blend all the ingredients together in the bowl with a wooden spoon (or place them in a food processor for a smoother consistency). Place the fruited butter into a small serving bowl or crock, cover it well, and refrigerate.

SERVICE Bring the butter to room temperature before serving.

Anyone can barbecue chicken or steak,

but Barbecued Polenta with zesty Tomato Pesto will earn you

the title "Vegetarian Host of the Year." The addition of Wild Mushroom

Chive Ragù steeped in white wine and butter enriches the flavors

of the grilled polenta.

The perfect accompaniments to the polenta

are a bread salad tossed with crisp summer vegetables and

the Lemon-Scented Chickpea and Zucchini Salad, both of

which add depth and balance to the entire menu.

Vegetarian Supper on the Grill

MENU

HORS D'OEUVRE SUGGESTION
Green Gazpacho Shots (page 20)

**BARBECUED POLENTA WITH
TOMATO PESTO AND MUSHROOM
CHIVE RAGÙ**

**LEMON-SCENTED CHICKPEA
AND ZUCCHINI SALAD**

BREAD SALAD WITH FRIED TOFU

DESSERT SUGGESTION
Intensely Moist Triple Chocolate Cake
with Fresh Berries and Cream (page 266)

WINE SUGGESTION: RED
Shiraz, Côtes du Rhône

Barbecued Polenta with Tomato Pesto and Mushroom Chive Ragù

KITCHENWARE
chef's knife, baking sheet,
medium saucepan, whisk,
wooden spoon, pepper mill,
pastry brush, spatula

**PREPARATION
TIME**
10 minutes plus 2 hours
chilling time

COOKING TIME
20 minutes

3 ½ tablespoons extra virgin olive oil

1 small red onion, finely chopped

5 ½ cups vegetable broth, homemade or low-sodium canned

1 ¾ cups yellow cornmeal

2 tablespoons plus 2 teaspoons finely chopped fresh basil

¾ teaspoon salt

¼ teaspoon freshly ground pepper

Garnishes: 1 large head radicchio, cored, washed and
separated into leaves

6 sprigs fresh basil

1. Grease the sides and bottom of the baking sheet with ½ tablespoon of the oil.

2. Heat 1 tablespoon of the oil in the saucepan over medium heat and sauté the onion until it is translucent, 3 to 4 minutes.

3. Add the broth and bring the liquid to a boil over medium-high heat. Pour the cornmeal into the broth in a steady stream, blending and stirring it constantly with a wire whisk. Lower the heat to medium-low and simmer the polenta, stirring it often with a wooden spoon, until the mixture pulls away from the sides of the pan, 15 to 20 minutes.

4. Remove the polenta from the heat and blend in 2 tablespoons of the basil, the salt, and the pepper. Spread the polenta, ¾ inch thick, onto the prepared baking sheet. Cover and refrigerate it for 2 hours or overnight.

5. Light a charcoal grill and wait until the coals are gray, or preheat a gas grill.

6. Cut the chilled polenta into 2 × 2-inch squares. Combine the remaining 2 tablespoons of oil with the remaining 2 teaspoons of basil and brush both sides of each square. Grill the polenta uncovered over medium-hot coals until the bottoms are golden brown, 5 to 6 minutes. Turn the polenta squares over with a spatula, brush them again with the basil oil, and grill them until golden brown, 5 minutes more.

SERVICE   Cover the bottom of a serving tray with the radicchio leaves. Arrange the polenta squares over the radicchio and garnish them with the basil sprigs. Serve the polenta with the Tomato Pesto and Mushroom Chive Ragù on the side.

COOK'S TIPS   Nonvegetarians can try the grilled polenta with lamb, fish, or chicken and can substitute chicken broth for the vegetable broth. The polenta can also be browned under the broiler.

Tomato Pesto

KITCHENWARE
grater, chef's knife, food
processor, medium bowl,
wooden spoon, pepper mill

**PREPARATION
TIME**
20 minutes

DO-AHEAD
Make the pesto up to 4 days
ahead and store, covered, in
the refrigerator.

2 cups firmly packed fresh basil
½ cup finely grated Parmesan cheese
⅓ cup pine nuts
3 cloves garlic, coarsely chopped
¼ teaspoon salt
¼ cup extra virgin olive oil
5 plum tomatoes, seeded and finely chopped
Freshly ground pepper

1. Place the basil leaves, Parmesan, pine nuts, garlic, and salt in the bowl of the food processor fitted with the steel blade. Process until it is puréed. Slowly pour the oil through the feed tube and pulse the mixture until it is blended.

2. Spoon the pesto into the bowl and blend in the tomatoes with a wooden spoon. Season with pepper to taste.

SERVICE Serve the pesto with the Barbecued Polenta.

COOK'S TIPS Heat the pesto and spoon over hot pasta. Serve with a green salad and crisp bread. Pass extra Parmesan.

Mushroom Chive Ragù

KITCHENWARE
chef's knife, large skillet,
wooden spoon, pepper mill

**PREPARATION
TIME**
10 minutes

COOKING TIME
25 minutes

4 tablespoons ($\frac{1}{2}$ stick) unsalted butter
3 large shallots, finely chopped
2 pounds wild mushrooms, such as porcini, oyster, or cremini
$\frac{1}{2}$ cup white wine
3 tablespoons finely chopped fresh chives
$\frac{1}{2}$ teaspoon salt
$\frac{1}{4}$ teaspoon freshly ground pepper

1. Warm 1 tablespoon of the butter in the skillet over medium heat. Add the shallots and sauté until they have wilted, 3 to 4 minutes.

2. Place half the remaining butter in the same skillet and heat until it melts. Add half the mushrooms and sauté them, stirring occasionally with a wooden spoon, until they have softened and given up their juices, 5 to 7 minutes. Remove the mushrooms from the pan, add the remaining $1\frac{1}{2}$ tablespoons butter, and sauté the remaining mushrooms.

3. Turn the heat to high. Return the previously sautéed mushrooms and shallots to the pan, along with the wine, and cook, stirring the mushrooms briskly, until the liquid has evaporated, about 2 minutes. Add the chives and season the ragù with the salt and pepper.

SERVICE Serve the mushrooms with the Barbecued Polenta.

COOK'S TIPS Try the mushrooms with scrambled eggs or as a topping for pasta tossed with olive oil and garlic.

Lemon-Scented Chickpea and Zucchini Salad

KITCHENWARE

chef's knife, zester, colander, large saucepan, medium saucepan, whisk, salad bowl, pepper mill, wooden spoons

PREPARATION TIME

20 minutes plus 30 minutes standing time

COOKING TIME

1 hour 20 minutes (or none, if using canned beans)

DO-AHEAD

Make the salad in the morning and refrigerate it, covered with plastic wrap. Bring it to room temperature and add the parsley just before serving.

¾ pound dried chickpeas, soaked overnight in water, or three 15-ounce cans, drained and rinsed (see Note)

¼ teaspoon table salt

4 medium-thin zucchini, trimmed

1 small red onion, finely chopped

2 medium cloves garlic, finely minced

1 teaspoon ground cumin

Zest and juice of 1 large lemon

½ cup extra virgin olive oil

1 ½ teaspoons kosher salt

Freshly ground pepper

Garnish: 2 tablespoons chopped fresh flat-leaf parsley

1. If starting with soaked dried chickpeas, drain them in a colander and place in the large saucepan with cold water to cover. Bring the water to a boil over high heat, lower the heat to medium, and simmer the chickpeas, uncovered, until they have softened but remain firm to the bite, about 70 minutes. After 1 hour of cooking, add the table salt. Drain the chickpeas in a colander and set them aside at room temperature.

2. Cut the zucchini in half lengthwise, then slice each half into ⅛-inch-thick half moons. Bring 3 quarts of water to a boil in the medium saucepan over high heat. Add the

zucchini, immediately turn the heat to low, and simmer the vegetable for 30 seconds. Drain the zucchini in a colander and shock it with cold water. Set it aside at room temperature and allow it to drain further.

3. Whisk together the onion, garlic, cumin, lemon zest and juice, oil, kosher salt, and pepper in the bottom of a salad bowl. Using two wooden spoons, gently toss the chickpeas and zucchini with the dressing. Make sure to coat the salad well with all the dressing. Reseason it, if necessary, with kosher salt and pepper.

SERVICE Let the salad stand at room temperature for 30 minutes to blend all the flavors. Just before serving, toss the salad with the parsley.

Note: If using canned chickpeas, do not cook them or add salt.

Bread Salad with Fried Tofu

KITCHENWARE

chef's knife, peeler, whisk, small bowl, pepper mill, large salad bowl and wooden salad servers, baking sheet, large nonstick skillet, metal spoon or tongs, slotted spoon, paper toweling

PREPARATION TIME

30 minutes

MARINATING TIME

1 hour

COOKING TIME

12 minutes for croutons, 5 minutes for tofu

DO-AHEAD

Prepare the salad through Step 5 early in the day and refrigerate.

THE SALAD DRESSING

¼ cup red wine vinegar

1 tablespoon finely chopped fresh oregano

1 teaspoon finely chopped fresh flat-leaf parsley

1 large clove garlic, finely minced

⅔ cup extra virgin olive oil

Salt and freshly ground pepper

THE SALAD

2 yellow bell peppers, cored, seeded, and cut into small dice

2 orange bell peppers, cored, seeded, and cut into small dice

2 large cucumbers, peeled, seeded and cut into small dice

4 scallions, cut into ⅛-inch-thick rounds

1 ½ cups fresh bean sprouts, rinsed and drained

1 tablespoon capers, rinsed, drained, and coarsely chopped

One 10-ounce loaf country-style or French bread, cut into 1-inch cubes (about 3 ½ cups)

6 tablespoons extra virgin olive oil

8 ounces firm tofu, cut into 1-inch cubes, patted dry on paper toweling

Salt and freshly ground pepper

1 small head romaine lettuce, cored and torn into bite-size pieces

1. **Make the dressing:** Whisk the vinegar, oregano, parsley, and garlic together in the small bowl. Gradually add the oil, whisking and blending the ingredients well. Season the dressing with salt and pepper to taste.

2. **Make the salad:** Combine the bell peppers, cucumbers, scallions, bean sprouts, and capers in the salad bowl.

3. Add the salad dressing, toss the vegetables to coat, and let marinate for 1 hour, covered, in the refrigerator.

4. Preheat the oven to 350 degrees.

5. Toss the bread cubes with 3 tablespoons of the oil and spread them loosely on the baking sheet. Bake the cubes, stirring occasionally, 12 to 15 minutes, until they are crisp and lightly browned. Cool them to room temperature.

6. Heat the remaining 3 tablespoons oil over medium heat in the skillet. Add the tofu and cook, stirring gently with a metal spoon or tongs, until it is golden on all sides. Remove the tofu with a slotted spoon and drain it on paper toweling. Season it with salt and pepper to taste and cool to room temperature.

SERVICE   Remove the salad from the refrigerator 10 minutes before serving. Add the bread cubes and tofu, and toss well with wooden salad servers. Just before serving, toss the salad with the romaine lettuce and season it again with salt and pepper.

COOK'S TIP   Add 4 tomatoes, cut into medium chunks, and 2 teaspoons of chopped fresh basil to the salad for a savory variation. At the same time, reduce the oregano by 1 teaspoon and the bell peppers to 1 each.

CHAPTER 4

Fall Menus

A Fall Seafood Ragoût

Rock Cornish Hen Thanksgiving

A Hearty Short Rib Dinner

An Informal Fall Pasta Dinner

A Heartwarming Vegetarian Soup and Sides

Shrimp and scallops, lightly marinated
in olive oil, garlic, and lime juice, served in a sauce of sautéed
fennel, scallions, tomatoes, cumin, and cilantro, create
a seafood dish loaded with eclectic Asian flavors.
Brown rice, simmered in white wine and vegetable broth
and surrounded with green onions, is the perfect accompaniment,
balancing the brilliant spices in the ragoût.
Combine lemon, shallots, and mustard with the crisp,
subtle flavor of two colors of beans for a salad with just the right
finishing touch. A bread bursting with the flavors of olives, tomato,
and oregano, along with the crunch of poppy seeds, brings
warmth to this fall menu.

A Fall Seafood Ragoût

MENU

HORS D'OEUVRE SUGGESTION
Prosciutto Tortilla Roulades with Dried Fig Jam (page 29)

SHRIMP AND SCALLOP RAGOÛT

BROWN RICE AND GREEN ONIONS

YELLOW WAX AND GREEN BEANS
IN SHALLOT AND MUSTARD VINAIGRETTE

TOMATO AND OLIVE BREAD

DESSERT SUGGESTION
Citrus Pound Cake with Brandied Raisins (page 262)

WINE SUGGESTION: WHITE
Pinot Grigio, Sauvignon Blanc

Shrimp and Scallop Ragoût

6 tablespoons extra virgin olive oil

2 medium cloves garlic, minced

Juice of 1 medium lime

1 pound large shrimp (21 to 25 count), peeled and deveined

1 pound sea scallops

1 medium fennel bulb, top and bottom removed, quartered and cut into $\frac{1}{2}$-inch dice

6 scallions, washed, trimmed, and finely chopped

2 large ripe tomatoes (about 2 pounds), peeled, seeded, and coarsely chopped

1 cup clam juice

$\frac{1}{2}$ cup dry white wine

$\frac{3}{4}$ teaspoon ground cumin seeds

1 small lemon, quartered

1 tablespoon finely chopped fresh cilantro

1 teaspoon salt

$\frac{1}{2}$ teaspoon freshly ground pepper

Garnish: 1 to 2 tablespoons chopped fresh cilantro

1. Whisk together 3 tablespoons of the oil, the garlic, and the lime juice in the small bowl. Toss the shrimp and scallops with the marinade, cover lightly, and marinate for 30 minutes in the refrigerator.

2. While the seafood is marinating, heat the remaining oil over medium heat in the saucepan. Add the fennel and sauté, stirring often, until it is translucent, 3 to 5 minutes. Add the scallions and continue to sauté the mixture 1 minute more.

3. Blend the tomatoes, clam juice, wine, cumin, and lemon with the fennel mixture. Simmer the sauce, uncovered, over medium heat for 20 minutes. Remove and discard the lemon. Add 1 tablespoon cilantro, salt, and pepper, and simmer 5 minutes more.

4. Remove the seafood from the marinade with a slotted spoon and set aside in the medium bowl. Heat the marinade in the skillet and sauté the shrimp and scallops in the marinade over medium-high heat, stirring often, until the seafood is translucent, about 2 minutes. (The shrimp and scallops will be undercooked.)

SERVICE   Gently combine the seafood with the sauce. About 10 minutes before serving, set the saucepan over medium-low heat and simmer the ragoût until hot, about 10 minutes. Sprinkle with the cilantro garnish just before serving.

COOK'S TIP   To give the sauce a savory taste, add ½ pound of sautéed sliced wild mushrooms.

Brown Rice and Green Onions

KITCHENWARE

chef's knife, medium saucepan
with cover, pepper mill

**PREPARATION
TIME**

10 minutes

COOKING TIME

50 minutes

DO-AHEAD

Chop the garlic and scallions
up to 1 day ahead. Store them
separately, covered, in the
refrigerator.

2 tablespoons unsalted butter

1 tablespoon extra virgin olive oil

2 cups brown rice

6 to 8 scallions, finely chopped

2 large cloves garlic, finely chopped

$\frac{1}{3}$ cup dry white wine

$4\frac{1}{2}$ cups low-sodium vegetable broth

1 tablespoon finely chopped fresh flat-leaf parsley

Salt and freshly ground pepper

1. Heat the butter and oil in the saucepan over medium heat. Add the rice and sauté 4 minutes, stirring often, until the rice is no longer opaque. Mix in the scallions and cook 2 minutes. Add the garlic and continue to cook 1 minute more.

2. Add the wine and vegetable broth and bring the mixture to a boil over high heat. Immediately lower the heat to medium-low and simmer the rice, covered, for about 45 minutes, or according to the instructions on the package, until all the liquid has been absorbed.

3. Blend the parsley with the rice and season it with salt and pepper to taste.

SERVICE Spoon the rice into a deep serving bowl, preferably not white.

COOK'S TIPS When finished, enhance the rice with 1 pound of cooked medium shrimp and ½ pound of cooked sea scallops for an easy supper entrée. Green salad and crisp warm bread complete the menu.

Yellow Wax and Green Beans in Shallot and Mustard Vinaigrette

KITCHENWARE
chef's knife, large saucepan, colander, food processor, pepper mill

PREPARATION TIME
10 minutes

COOKING TIME
4 to 5 minutes

DO-AHEAD
The beans and vinaigrette can be made the day before. Store them separately, covered, in the refrigerator. Bring the beans to room temperature before adding the vinaigrette.

1 pound young yellow wax beans, trimmed
1 pound young green beans, trimmed
2 tablespoons fresh lemon juice
1 tablespoon red wine vinegar
1 teaspoon whole-grain mustard
½ cup extra virgin olive oil
1 medium shallot, finely minced
1 teaspoon salt
¼ teaspoon freshly ground pepper

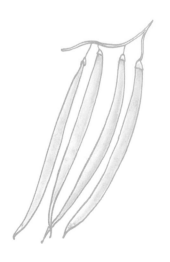

1. Bring 6 quarts of lightly salted water to a boil over high heat in the saucepan. Add the wax and green beans. Lower the heat to medium and cook the beans, uncovered, until they are crisp to the bite, about 4 minutes. Drain the beans and shock them in cold water to stop the cooking; drain them again, and reserve them at room temperature. *(If the beans are not uniform in size, cook them in two separate saucepans.)*

2. Put the lemon juice, vinegar, and mustard in the bowl of the food processor fitted with the steel blade and process to blend the ingredients.

3. With the food processor motor running, add the oil slowly through the feed tube until the dressing has thickened. Stir in the shallot and season the vinaigrette with the salt and pepper.

SERVICE   Toss the beans with the vinaigrette 20 minutes before serving. The beans taste best served at room temperature.

COOK'S TIPS   Sauté ½ pound of diced pancetta until crisp. Drain it well and add it to the beans for a hearty accompaniment to simple pasta or broiled fish dinners. If you are unable to find yellow wax beans, double the quantity of green beans.

Tomato and Olive Bread

KITCHENWARE

9-inch loaf pan, food processor, greased large bowl, plastic wrap or kitchen towel, pastry brush, rack

PREPARATION TIME

30 minutes plus 1½ hours rising time

COOKING TIME

45 minutes

DO-AHEAD

Chop the tomatoes and olives up to 1 day ahead and store them separately, covered, in the refrigerator.

1 tablespoon active dry yeast

2 tablespoons honey

2 teaspoons salt

¾ cup whole wheat flour

1 cup canned plum tomatoes with their juice, chopped medium

2 tablespoons extra virgin olive oil

1 tablespoon finely chopped fresh oregano

1 tablespoon plus ¼ teaspoon poppy seeds

2½ to 3 cups all-purpose flour

15 Greek olives, pitted and chopped medium

1 tablespoon unsalted butter, melted

1. Grease the loaf pan.

2. Dissolve the yeast and honey in ½ cup warm water in the bowl of the food processor. This allows the yeast to proof.

3. Add the salt, whole wheat flour, tomatoes, oil, oregano, and 1 tablespoon of the poppy seeds to the yeast mixture. Pulse the mixture, using the steel blade, until the ingredients are blended.

4. Add 2½ cups of the all-purpose flour and process, using more flour as needed, until the dough forms a sticky ball and leaves the sides of the bowl. Turn the it onto a lightly floured board and knead in the olives, adding more flour

as necessary. Put the dough into the large bowl, cover with plastic wrap, and allow it to rise until doubled in volume, about 1 hour.

5. Lightly flour your fingertips. Punch the dough down on a floured surface and knead it for 5 strokes. Shape the dough into a loaf and place it in the prepared loaf pan. Cover the top lightly with plastic wrap or a damp kitchen towel and allow it to rise for 30 minutes in a warm place.

6. Preheat the oven to 350 degrees.

7. Brush the top of the bread with the butter and sprinkle it with the remaining poppy seeds. Bake the bread for 45 minutes, or until the top is crusty and lightly browned. Remove the loaf from the pan to a rack and cool.

SERVICE The flavors of the bread are really startling when it is served warm. If the cholesterol count doesn't get in the way, serve the bread with a crock of unsalted butter. Using a serrated knife makes slicing very easy.

COOK'S TIP For variety, add two freshly chopped large cloves garlic and ¼ cup walnut pieces to the batter in Step 4.

Instead of serving the traditional roast turkey
for Thanksgiving, surprise your guests with intensely flavored,
crisp Rock Cornish hens steeped in a fragrant marinade. The earthy taste
of mushrooms and the sharp flavor of balsamic vinegar in the sauce are
gentled by the addition of sour cream. Accompany the Slavic-inspired
hens with a combination of kasha (or buckwheat groats), yams, and
butternut squash for a "taste of Russia."
If you are not yet an aficionado of beets, roasting them with
caraway butter will make you a fan. They are sweet, earthy, piquant,
and unbelievably simple to prepare.
Crisp sliced cucumbers dressed in a light red wine vinaigrette
not only add contrast to the menu but are
refreshing and stimulating as well.

Rock Cornish Hen Thanksgiving

MENU

HORS D'OEUVRE SUGGESTION
Miniature Eggplant Crisps (page 27)

ROCK CORNISH HENS, CHUNKY MUSHROOMS, AND SOUR CREAM

BUCKWHEAT GROATS WITH BUTTERNUT SQUASH AND YAMS

ROASTED BEETS WITH CARAWAY BUTTER (PAGE 94)

CUCUMBER AND RED ONION SALAD WITH CHIVES AND DILL

DESSERT SUGGESTION
Chocolate Chocolate Chip Banana Ice Cream Cake
with Pecan Rum Caramel Sauce (page 257)

WINE SUGGESTION: RED
Rioja, Red Zinfandel

Rock Cornish Hens, Chunky Mushrooms, and Sour Cream

KITCHENWARE
chef's knife, small bowl, large noncorrosive baking pan, large skillet, medium skillet, aluminum foil, pepper mill

PREPARATION TIME
20 minutes

MARINATING TIME
6 hours or overnight

COOKING TIME
1 hour

DO-AHEAD
Chop the onion and garlic up to 1 day ahead and store them, separately, covered, in the refrigerator.

1 medium Spanish onion, finely chopped

2 medium cloves garlic, finely chopped

2 teaspoons finely chopped fresh tarragon

6 tablespoons extra virgin olive oil

3 Rock Cornish hens (about 1 ½ pounds each), quartered (see Note)

1 cup chicken broth, homemade or low-sodium canned

1 cup dry white wine

2 tablespoons unsalted butter

1 pound domestic or wild mushrooms, washed, dried, and quartered

½ teaspoon finely chopped fresh sage

1 tablespoon balsamic vinegar

½ cup sour cream

1 tablespoon finely chopped fresh flat-leaf parsley

Salt and freshly ground pepper

Garnish: 6 sprigs fresh tarragon

1. Combine the onion, garlic, tarragon, and 3 tablespoons of the oil in the small bowl. Arrange the hens in the baking pan and rub each piece with the marinade, using it all. Refrigerate the hens, covered, for 6 hours or overnight.

2. Preheat the oven to 350 degrees.

3. Heat the remaining 3 tablespoons oil in the large skillet over medium heat. Sauté the hen pieces on both sides, skin side down first, until they are golden brown.

4. Put the hens in the baking pan, skin side up. Add the chicken broth and wine and roast for 45 to 50 minutes, until they are cooked through. (When the hens are done, the juices will run clear when a thigh is pierced with the tines of a fork.)

5. While the hens are roasting, heat the butter in the medium skillet over medium heat and sauté the mushrooms with the sage until they are golden brown, about 5 minutes. Add the vinegar and cook about 30 seconds longer, until the vinegar has evaporated.

6. When the hens are finished roasting, transfer them to a serving platter and cover them lightly with aluminum foil. Pour the drippings from the roasting pan into the skillet with the mushrooms, blending well. With the heat on low, add the sour cream slowly, stirring constantly until it is blended with the sauce. Add the parsley and season with salt and pepper to taste. Be sure to keep the heat low, because sour cream curdles over high heat.

SERVICE Garnish the hens with the tarragon sprigs and serve them with a sauceboat of the chunky mushrooms on the side.

COOK'S TIPS Add 2 peeled and chopped tomatoes to the mushrooms before adding the sour cream. The mushrooms are a hearty addition to beef pot roast or pasta tossed with olive oil and Parmesan cheese. Remember to reheat a sauce made with sour cream over medium-low heat so that it doesn't curdle.

Note: Cornish hens are traditionally sold whole. Ask your butcher to cut them into quarters.

Buckwheat Groats with Butternut Squash and Yams

KITCHENWARE
chef's knife, zester, medium saucepan, large skillet, medium bowl, large baking sheet, spatula, pepper mill

PREPARATION TIME
20 minutes

COOKING TIME
50 minutes

DO-AHEAD
Chop the onion 1 day ahead and store it, covered, in the refrigerator.

2 ¾ cups chicken broth, homemade or low-sodium canned
1 cup buckwheat groats (kasha)
2 tablespoons unsalted butter
1 medium onion, finely chopped
2 yams, peeled and cut into ¼-inch dice
1 butternut squash (about 1 pound), peeled, seeded, and cut into ¼-inch dice
2 tablespoons extra virgin olive oil
½ teaspoon salt
¼ teaspoon freshly ground pepper
Garnish: ½ teaspoon orange zest

1. Bring 2 cups of the chicken broth to a boil over medium-high heat in the saucepan. Add the buckwheat groats, lower the heat to medium-low, and simmer the grain, covered, for 15 minutes, until all the liquid has been absorbed. Uncover, fluff the grains with a fork, and set aside at room temperature.

2. Heat the butter in the skillet over medium-high heat. Add the onion and sauté, stirring occasionally, until golden brown and caramelized, 12 to 15 minutes.

3. Preheat the oven to 400 degrees.

4. Toss the yams and squash in the bowl with the oil. Place the vegetables on the baking sheet and roast them for 20 to 25 minutes, or until fork tender. After 10 to 15 minutes, rotate the pan or turn the vegetables with a spatula.

5. Combine the onion and vegetables with the buckwheat groats and add the salt and pepper.

SERVICE The colors of the buckwheat groats, squash, and yams look brilliant served from a copper pan or in colorful pottery. Sprinkle the top with the orange zest before serving.

COOK'S TIP 1 pound of medium-chopped mushrooms can be sautéed with the onion and blended into the buckwheat groats in place of the squash and yams. Season the dish with ½ teaspoon fresh thyme.

Cucumber and Red Onion Salad with Chives and Dill

KITCHENWARE

chef's knife, paring knife, 3 small bowls, whisk

PREPARATION TIME

30 minutes

REFRIGERATION TIME

30 minutes

DO-AHEAD

All the vegetables can be prepared early in the day. Store them separately, covered, in the refrigerator.

2 pounds young cucumbers

1 small red onion, cut into $1/8$-inch-thick slices

1 small red bell pepper, cored, seeded, and diced small

1 small yellow bell pepper, cored, seeded, and diced small

2 teaspoons sugar

2 teaspoons sherry wine vinegar

2 tablespoons extra virgin olive oil

2 tablespoons thinly sliced fresh chives, about $1/8$-inch-thick rounds

1 teaspoon finely chopped fresh dill

$1/2$ teaspoon salt

$1/4$ teaspoon ground white pepper

1. Peel and slice the cucumbers into $1/8$-inch-thick rounds. *(If the cucumber seeds are large, remove them with a melon baller, then slice the cucumber halves.)* Refrigerate the cucumber slices for 30 minutes, lightly covered.

2. Separate the onion slices into rings. Refrigerate the onion rings and bell peppers separately for 30 minutes.

3. Combine the sugar, vinegar, and olive oil in a small bowl.

SERVICE Arrange the cucumber slices in concentric circles on a 10- to 12-inch flat glass or pottery plate. Scatter the onion rings randomly over the cucumbers. Scatter the bell peppers over the onion rings. Sprinkle the chives, dill, salt, and white pepper over the vegetables. Whisk the dressing and spoon it over the salad.

COOK'S TIP Add 2 large diced tomatoes to the cucumber salad and substitute tarragon for the dill.

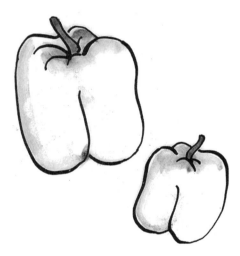

If you're tired of battling over the succulent
bones of a prime rib, braised short ribs are the answer. They provide
the same irresistible dining experience as a prime rib roast, plus there
are more than enough bones for everyone. A perfect match for these
braised ribs is the Caramelized Onion Horseradish Sauce. The debate,
however, is how much horseradish to add to the sauce to make it just right.
The answer is up to you. Enjoy experimenting and create
your own balance of tastes.
Buttery, creamy mashed potatoes blended with subtle, earthy parsnips
make the ultimate comfort food accompaniment.
Colorful, crunchy carrot and zucchini pancakes, heated
with a dash of cayenne, balance the menu. (You can also make
these pancakes smaller and serve them as an
hors d'oeuvre during cocktail hour.)
Then refresh the palate with a salad of butter lettuce mixed
with crisp celery and dressed in a nutty vinaigrette.
A final note: For those who pick up the short ribs,
a basket of moist towelettes is de rigueur.

A Hearty Short Rib Dinner

MENU

HORS D'OEUVRE SUGGESTION
Asian-Spiced Scallop Saté (page 10)

BRAISED SHORT RIBS OF BEEF
WITH CARAMELIZED ONION HORSERADISH SAUCE

MASHED POTATOES, PARSNIPS, AND SOUR CREAM

CARROT AND ZUCCHINI PANCAKES

BUTTER LETTUCE WITH TANGERINES, CELERY, AND WALNUT VINAIGRETTE

DESSERT SUGGESTION
Cheddar Cheese Crusted Apple Pie (page 254)

WINE SUGGESTION: RED
Merlot, Cabernet Sauvignon

Braised Short Ribs of Beef with Caramelized Onion Horseradish Sauce

KITCHENWARE
chef's knife, peeler, pepper mill, large roasting pan, large platter, aluminum foil, slotted spoon, food processor, medium saucepan

PREPARATION TIME
1 hour

COOKING TIME
3 hours

DO-AHEAD
All the vegetables can be prepared the day before. Store them separately, covered, in the refrigerator.

8 pounds short ribs of beef

1 teaspoon salt

$\frac{1}{2}$ teaspoon freshly ground pepper

$\frac{1}{4}$ cup extra virgin olive oil

3 large Spanish onions, chopped medium

6 large shallots, chopped medium

4 large carrots, trimmed, peeled, and chopped medium

4 celery ribs, trimmed and chopped medium

6 large cloves garlic, chopped medium

6 cups low-sodium beef broth

4 cups full-bodied red wine, such as Zinfandel or Cabernet

$\frac{1}{2}$ teaspoon finely chopped fresh thyme

$\frac{1}{2}$ teaspoon finely chopped fresh rosemary

1 recipe Caramelized Onion Horseradish Sauce (recipe follows)

1. Preheat the oven to 350 degrees.

2. Rub the beef ribs with the salt and pepper. Heat the oil in the roasting pan over medium-high heat on top of the stove. When the oil is hot, add the ribs and brown them on all sides. Transfer the browned ribs to the platter.

3. Add the onions, shallots, carrots, and celery to the oil remaining in the roasting pan and sauté over medium-

high heat until they are soft and the onions are golden, about 10 minutes. Add the garlic and cook 1 minute more.

4. Add the beef broth, wine, thyme, and rosemary to the pan. Stir well and bring the liquid to a simmer on top of the stove. Return the beef ribs to the roasting pan; cover the pan tightly with aluminum foil, and transfer it to the oven. Braise the ribs for 2 hours. (Make certain that the liquid in the roasting pan simmers slowly. Lower the heat to 325 degrees if the liquid is cooking too fast.) The short ribs are ready when the meat is fork tender and has started to recede from the bones.

5. Using a slotted spoon, transfer the vegetables from the roasting pan to a food processor fitted with the steel blade. Add 1 ½ cups of the pan liquid, and process until the vegetables are puréed. Pour the remaining liquid and the puréed vegetables into the saucepan and simmer the sauce over medium heat until it has reduced and thickened, 10 to 12 minutes. Season it with salt and pepper to taste.

6. Pour the sauce over the ribs and cook them in the oven for 30 minutes longer.

SERVICE   Serve the ribs in individual shallow bowls or arrange them on a large platter masked lightly with the sauce. Since the puréed vegetables have a tendency to drop to the bottom of the pan, make certain to mix the sauce well. Pour the remaining sauce into a sauceboat and pass it side by side with the Caramelized Onion Horseradish Sauce.

COOK'S TIP   For enhanced flavor, sauté 1 pound of shiitake or oyster mushrooms in 2 tablespoons of extra virgin olive oil and add them to the short rib sauce while it is reducing.

Caramelized Onion Horseradish Sauce

KITCHENWARE
chef's knife, medium skillet,
medium bowl, pepper mill

**PREPARATION
TIME**
10 minutes

COOKING TIME
20 minutes

DO-AHEAD
The sauce can be prepared up
to 1 day ahead and stored,
covered, in the refrigerator.

3 tablespoons unsalted butter
1 large onion, diced medium
¾ cup sour cream
¾ cup yogurt
1 teaspoon well-drained bottled white horseradish
½ teaspoon whole-grain mustard
Salt and freshly ground pepper

1. Heat the butter in the skillet over medium-low heat.
   Add the onion and cook slowly for 15 minutes, stirring
   occasionally. As the onion begins to turn golden and
   caramelize, stir it often to ensure that it browns evenly.
   Cook 4 to 6 minutes more, then set aside to cool at room
   temperature.

2. Blend the sour cream, yogurt, horseradish, and mustard together in the bowl. Add the cooled onion, season the sauce
   with salt and pepper to taste, and chill in the refrigerator.

SERVICE Spoon the tangy horseradish sauce into a vi-
brantly colored serving bowl and serve it with the Braised
Short Ribs of Beef.

COOK'S TIPS Be sure to serve the sauce lightly chilled to
thoroughly enjoy the tangy taste. If it is refrigerated
overnight, correct the seasonings before serving. Try this
sauce with roast lamb, pork, or grilled fish as well.

Mashed Potatoes, Parsnips, and Sour Cream

KITCHENWARE

chef's knife, peeler, 2 medium saucepans, colander, large mixing bowl, potato masher or ricer, pepper mill, 3½- to 4-quart baking dish

PREPARATION TIME

20 minutes

COOKING TIME

25 minutes

DO-AHEAD

Prepare the potatoes the day before, cover them with water, and store them, covered, in the refrigerator.

2 pounds Idaho potatoes, peeled and quartered

Salt and freshly ground pepper

1 pound parsnips, trimmed, peeled, and cut into 1-inch chunks

6 tablespoons unsalted butter, cut into small pieces, at room temperature

½ cup sour cream

1 tablespoon finely chopped fresh flat-leaf parsley

Garnish: 1 teaspoon finely chopped fresh flat-leaf parsley

1. Bring 3 quarts of water to a boil in a saucepan over high heat. Add the potatoes with a pinch of salt, lower the heat to medium, and simmer uncovered until they are fork tender, 10 to 15 minutes. Drain well and transfer them to the bowl.

2. While the potatoes are cooking, bring 2 quarts of water to a boil in the other saucepan over high heat. Add the parsnips with a pinch of salt, lower the heat to medium, and simmer uncovered until fork tender, 10 to 15 minutes. Drain well and add them to the potatoes.

3. Preheat the oven to 400 degrees.

4. Mash the potatoes and parsnips together with a potato masher or put them through a potato ricer. Add 4 tablespoons of the butter, the sour cream, and 1 tablespoon parsley and mix well until the potato-parsnip mixture has a smooth consistency. *(Do not purée the potato-parsnip mixture in a food processor. The consistency will become starchy and gluey.)* Season the mixture with salt and pepper to taste.

5. Spoon the potato-parsnip mixture into the baking dish. Dot the top with the remaining 2 tablespoons butter, and bake for 25 minutes, until the potatoes are bubbly and lightly browned. Keep the baking dish warm in a 250-degree oven for 15 to 20 minutes before serving.

SERVICE Serve the potatoes piping hot and dusted with the parsley garnish.

COOK'S TIP Add ½ teaspoon drained white horseradish to the vegetables as they are blended with the sour cream and butter for a bit of extra zip.

Carrot and Zucchini Pancakes

KITCHENWARE

peeler, paring knife, food processor or shredder, chef's knife, grater, large bowl, large heavy-bottomed skillet, slotted spoon, paper toweling, baking sheet

PREPARATION TIME

30 minutes

COOKING TIME

15 to 20 minutes

DO-AHEAD

These pancakes can be made the day before. Store them, covered, in the refrigerator. Bring them to room temperature and follow the warming instructions in Step 3.

2 medium carrots, trimmed, peeled, finely shredded, and squeezed dry

2 small zucchini, trimmed, finely shredded, and squeezed dry

2 large eggs, beaten

3 scallions, finely chopped

1 teaspoon grated ginger

1 teaspoon salt

⅛ teaspoon cayenne

⅓ cup all-purpose flour

3 tablespoons vegetable oil

Garnish: 1 teaspoon finely chopped fresh curly parsley

1. Combine the carrots, zucchini, eggs, scallions, ginger, salt, cayenne, and flour in the bowl.

2. Heat 1 tablespoon of the oil in the skillet over medium-high heat. To test for the correct seasoning in the pancakes, drop 1 tablespoon of batter into the oil and fry it 2 to 3 minutes. Taste and reseason the batter as necessary.

3. Drop heaping tablespoons of batter into the oil. Press the pancakes down with the back of a spoon, and fry them until they are golden brown, 2 to 3 minutes on each side. To ensure that the pancakes are crisp, fry them in small batches, and do not overcrowd the pan. After each batch, add 1 tablespoon oil. With a slotted spoon, place the pancakes on paper toweling as they are finished. Then transfer the pancakes to the baking sheet and keep them warm in a 300-degree oven for about 20 minutes.

SERVICE Arrange the pancakes in a flat basket lined with a colorful napkin and dust them with the parsley. The pancakes should be served warm so that they retain their crispness. If they are not piping hot, the taste will still be wonderful.

COOK'S TIP Grated butternut squash and beets also make colorful and delicious pancakes. Garnish them with 1 teaspoon orange zest instead of the parsley.

Butter Lettuce with Tangerines, Celery, and Walnut Vinaigrette

KITCHENWARE

**large salad bowl, food
processor**

PREPARATION
TIME

20 minutes

DO-AHEAD

**In the morning, prepare the
lettuce, tangerines, and celery,
and store them separately,
covered, in the refrigerator.
The dressing can also be made
in the morning and
refrigerated.**

3 small heads butter lettuce, cored and separated
    into leaves
3 tangerines or tangelos, peeled and sectioned,
    white pith removed
4 medium celery ribs, trimmed and thinly sliced crosswise
2 tablespoons finely chopped fresh chives
2 tablespoons fresh lemon juice
2 tablespoons fresh orange juice
$\frac{1}{2}$ cup walnut pieces
$\frac{1}{3}$ cup extra virgin olive oil
$\frac{1}{2}$ teaspoon salt
Pinch of cayenne (optional)
Garnish: 12 walnut halves

1. Toss the lettuce, tangerine sections, celery, and chives
   together in the salad bowl.

2. In the bowl of the food processor fitted with the steel
   blade, process the lemon juice, orange juice, and walnut
   pieces until smooth. Slowly add the olive oil through the
   feed tube until the dressing is creamy. Season the vinaigrette with the salt and the cayenne, if using.

SERVICE Toss the salad with the vinaigrette, season it
again, and garnish the top with the walnut halves.

Whole wheat pasta sauced with vegetables,
veal, white wine, and cream is the perfect menu to serve from
your kitchen counter. The intensity of fresh sage adds electricity to the
flavors of the pasta. The addition of rich Fontina cheese will have your guests
reaching for more.
Colorful red and yellow teardrop tomatoes go down like popcorn.
Once you have tasted the first one, the rest will disappear in rapid succession.
We eat them right out of the box and often forget about the recipe!
The Endive, Radicchio, and Gorgonzola Salad has a secret ingredient:
chopped hard-cooked eggs. Guests invariably ask, "What did you put in the
salad?" Don't tell them your culinary secret!
Oven-fresh biscuits complete this menu. Bake these delicious
Parsley and Basil Biscuits 45 minutes before dinner and keep
them in a warm place, covered with a kitchen towel
to retain their heat.

An Informal Fall Pasta Dinner

MENU

HORS D'OEUVRE SUGGESTION
Salt-Cured Cilantro-Rubbed Salmon on Cilantro Crostini
with Balsamic–Roasted Garlic Aioli Sauce (page 35)

WHOLE WHEAT PASTA WITH
VEAL, ZUCCHINI, AND FONTINA

RED AND YELLOW TEARDROP TOMATOES
WITH SHALLOTS

ENDIVE, RADICCHIO, AND GORGONZOLA
SALAD WITH BALSAMIC VINAIGRETTE

PARSLEY AND BASIL BISCUITS
WITH ROASTED GARLIC

DESSERT SUGGESTION
Intensely Moist Triple Chocolate Cake
with Fresh Berries and Cream (page 266)

WINE SUGGESTION: WHITE
Chardonnay

Whole Wheat Pasta with Veal, Zucchini, and Fontina

KITCHENWARE

chef's knife, peeler, grater, extra-large skillet or 14-inch sauté pan, wooden spoon, large saucepan, colander, small oven-to-table baking dish

PREPARATION TIME

15 minutes

COOKING TIME

1 hour

DO-AHEAD

This recipe can be made early in the day through Step 5, without baking. Store it, covered, in the refrigerator. Bring it to room temperature before baking as directed.

2 tablespoons extra virgin olive oil

2 medium onions, cut into $\frac{1}{4}$-inch dice

2 large carrots, trimmed, peeled, and cut into $\frac{1}{4}$-inch dice

2 celery ribs, trimmed and cut into $\frac{1}{4}$-inch dice

2 large zucchini, trimmed and cut into $\frac{1}{4}$-inch dice

3 large cloves garlic, cut into slivers

$1\frac{1}{2}$ pounds ground veal

$\frac{1}{2}$ cup dry white wine

$1\frac{1}{2}$ cups chicken broth, homemade or low-sodium canned

$\frac{1}{2}$ cup heavy cream

3 tablespoons minced fresh sage

3 tablespoons minced fresh flat-leaf parsley

$1\frac{3}{4}$ teaspoons salt

$\frac{1}{2}$ teaspoon white pepper

10 ounces whole wheat pasta, such as penne or orecchiette

$\frac{3}{4}$ cup freshly grated Fontina cheese

Garnish: 6 sprigs fresh sage

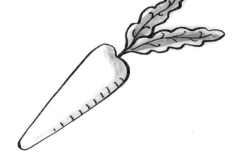

1. Heat the oil in the skillet and sauté the onions, carrots, and celery over medium heat for 5 to 8 minutes. Push the vegetables to the side with a wooden spoon and sauté the zucchini for 3 minutes. Push the zucchini to the side and sauté the garlic until it is golden, 1 to 2 minutes. Add the veal, breaking it into small pieces, and cook until all the pink has disappeared. Combine all the ingredients in the skillet with the wooden spoon.

2. Add the wine to the skillet and cook until it has almost evaporated, 5 to 8 minutes. Stir in the chicken broth, raise the heat to medium-high, and bring the liquid to a boil. Lower the heat to medium, add the cream, sage, parsley, 1½ teaspoons of the salt, and the pepper, and simmer until slightly thickened, 5 to 8 minutes.

3. Preheat the oven to 350 degrees.

4. Bring 3 quarts of water to a boil in the saucepan with the remaining ¼ teaspoon salt. Add the pasta and simmer it uncovered until just resistant to the bite (al dente), 6 to 8 minutes. Drain the pasta in the colander and heap it into the baking dish.

5. Combine the meat sauce, the pasta, and ½ cup of the Fontina. Season the dish again with salt and white pepper to taste. Sprinkle the remaining cheese over the pasta and bake for 30 minutes.

SERVICE Garnish with the sage sprigs and serve in the oven-to-table baking dish.

COOK'S TIPS If preparing the pasta early in the day, refrigerate in the baking dish, covered. Then bring to room temperature and bake as directed. Ground lamb or turkey can be substituted for the veal. Substitute fresh rosemary for the sage.

Red and Yellow Teardrop Tomatoes with Shallots

KITCHENWARE
chef's knife, serrated knife,
large sauté pan, wooden spoon

PREPARATION
TIME
20 minutes

COOKING TIME
5 minutes

2 pints red teardrop tomatoes

2 pints yellow teardrop tomatoes

2 tablespoons extra virgin olive oil

2 large shallots, finely chopped

1 teaspoon balsamic vinegar

¼ teaspoon red pepper flakes

1 teaspoon salt

Garnish: 1 tablespoon finely chopped fresh chives

1. Slice the tomatoes in half lengthwise with a serrated knife.

2. Heat the oil in the sauté pan over medium heat and sauté the shallots until they are soft and translucent, about 2 minutes. Raise the heat to medium-high, add the tomatoes, and sauté, tossing with a wooden spoon, until they are warmed through, about 3 minutes.

3. Blend the vinegar and red pepper flakes with the tomatoes and season with the salt.

SERVICE These dazzling red and yellow tomatoes look elegant in a black serving bowl. Any dark pottery that offers a contrast is fun to use. Sprinkle the tomatoes with the chives just before serving, and serve them warm.

COOK'S TIPS Cherry tomatoes or grape tomatoes are good substitutes for the teardrops. If the tomatoes are large, cut them in quarters instead of halves.

Endive, Radicchio, and Gorgonzola Salad with Balsamic Vinaigrette

KITCHENWARE
sharp kitchen knife, medium wooden or pottery salad bowl, pepper mill

PREPARATION TIME
15 minutes

COOKING TIME
10 to 12 minutes for the eggs

DO-AHEAD
Prepare the endive no more than 1 hour before using, as it tends to turn brown when exposed to the air.

3 large heads Belgian endive
3 small heads radicchio
2 hard-cooked eggs
1 recipe Balsamic Vinaigrette (recipe follows)
3 ounces crumbled Gorgonzola cheese
Freshly ground pepper

1. Cut the endives into quarters. Remove and discard the cores, and cut each quarter into $\frac{1}{8}$-inch julienne strips.

2. Cut the radicchio in quarters. Remove and discard the cores. Slice the radicchio into $\frac{1}{8}$-inch julienne strips.

3. Chop the hard-cooked eggs with a sharp knife until they are finely minced. Set them aside, covered, at room temperature. (*Eggs chopped in the food processor will turn into paste very quickly.*)

SERVICE Toss the endive and radicchio with the Balsamic Vinaigrette in the salad bowl. Sprinkle the hard-cooked eggs over the salad, then scatter the Gorgonzola over the eggs. The salad can also be arranged the same way and served on individual plates. Pass the pepper mill.

COOK'S TIPS Adding $\frac{1}{2}$ cup of chopped walnuts or pecans gives the salad extra crunch.

Balsamic Vinaigrette

KITCHENWARE

chef's knife, food processor, whisk

PREPARATION TIME

15 minutes

DO-AHEAD

Since this vinaigrette does not emulsify well, prepare it no more than a few hours before serving.

1 large clove garlic, coarsely chopped

1 teaspoon chopped fresh basil

1 teaspoon chopped fresh thyme

1 teaspoon Dijon mustard

1 tablespoon fresh lemon juice

2 teaspoons balsamic vinegar

½ cup extra virgin olive oil

½ teaspoon salt

¼ teaspoon freshly ground pepper

1. Put the garlic, basil, thyme, mustard, lemon juice, and vinegar in the bowl of the food processor fitted with the steel blade. Pulse until the ingredients are puréed. With the motor running, slowly pour the oil through the feed tube until the dressing is thickened.

2. Season the vinaigrette with the salt and pepper.

3. Whisk the dressing to reblend all the ingredients just before serving.

Parsley and Basil Biscuits with Roasted Garlic

KITCHENWARE

chef's knife, grater, food
processor or pastry cutter,
large bowl, wooden spoon,
parchment paper–lined baking
sheet, rack

PREPARATION
TIME

30 minutes plus roasting time
for garlic

COOKING TIME

12 minutes

DO-AHEAD

Roast garlic up to 1 day ahead.
Store, covered, in the
refrigerator.

3 ¼ cups self-rising flour

1 teaspoon baking powder

1 cup grated Asiago cheese

6 tablespoons vegetable shortening

1 tablespoon finely chopped fresh curly parsley

1 tablespoon finely chopped fresh basil

1 small head roasted garlic finely mashed (see page 286) at
   room temperature

1 ½ cups buttermilk

Egg Wash (see page 285)

1. Preheat the oven to 450 degrees.

2. Place 3 cups of the flour and the baking powder in the
   bowl of the food processor fitted with the steel blade and
   process for 15 to 20 seconds. Add the Asiago and shortening and pulse until the mixture resembles coarse meal.
   Add the parsley, basil, and garlic and pulse just enough
   to mix. Turn the batter into the bowl and mix in the
   buttermilk with a wooden spoon until just blended.

3. Drop the batter by spoonfuls onto the baking sheet.

4. Brush the biscuits with egg wash and bake them for
   about 12 minutes, until the tops are golden brown. Cool
   on a rack.

SERVICE Put the biscuits in a napkin-lined basket or bread tray. Double the recipe for friends with hearty appetites and be assured all the biscuits will disappear. Be extravagant and put a crock of butter on the table. It's well worth the calories.

COOK'S TIP For mouth-watering biscuits, brush the tops with melted butter as they emerge from the oven.

No one can resist rich, thick, intense

black bean soup scented with a combination of cilantro,

cumin, coriander, and oregano. This is a perfect menu to serve after

an afternoon of serious physical activity. You'll replace the energy

you've expended and eat "healthy" at the same time.

Balance the intensity of the soup with roasted bell peppers filled with

creamy ricotta cheese and chewy Monterey Jack. The piquant flavor of

jalapeño adds a bit of hot spice to the recipe.

Its crunchy texture and citrus flavor make the Red and White

Cabbage Slaw a perfect foil for the soup.

Ruby Grapefruit Salad with Radicchio and Watercress completes the meal.

The pink juicy citrus is the perfect complement to the intense flavors

of the soup and the roasted bell peppers.

Use crockery of different shapes and sizes for this menu.

Orange, yellow, rust, and green napkins and flowers, plus chunky candles

in fall colors, complete the picture.

A Heartwarming Vegetarian
Soup and Sides

MENU

HORS D'OEUVRE SUGGESTION
Portobello Steak Fries with
Balsamic–Roasted Garlic Aioli Sauce (page 32)

SERIOUSLY THICK BLACK BEAN SOUP

**ROASTED BELL PEPPERS FILLED WITH
CHEESE AND JALAPEÑO CHILES**

RED AND WHITE CABBAGE SLAW

**RUBY GRAPEFRUIT SALAD
WITH RADICCHIO AND WATERCRESS
(PAGE 48)**

DESSERT SUGGESTION
Blackberry Brandy Fresh Plum Bread Pudding (page 252)

WINE SUGGESTION: RED
Merlot, Pinot Noir

Seriously Thick Black Bean Soup

KITCHENWARE
chef's knife, large stockpot,
food processor, pepper mill

**PREPARATION
TIME**
30 minutes

COOKING TIME
2½ hours

DO-AHEAD
Prepare the onion, garlic, and
bell pepper the day before and
store them separately,
covered, in the refrigerator.
The soup can be made early in
the day, stored at room
temperature, and reheated
before serving.

1 pound dried black beans

2 bay leaves

1 medium Spanish onion, chopped medium

4 large cloves garlic, coarsely chopped

1 green bell pepper, cored, seeded, and chopped medium

1 bunch fresh cilantro, washed, large stems removed

1 teaspoon ground cumin

1 teaspoon ground coriander

1 teaspoon dried Mexican oregano (found in the Mexican
   foods aisle in supermarkets)

½ cup tomato purée

2 teaspoons salt

1 teaspoon freshly ground pepper

Garnishes: 3 tablespoons sour cream

2 tablespoons finely chopped red onion

1. Rinse the beans well in cold water and sort, discarding any that are shriveled. Bring 6 quarts of cold water to a boil in the stockpot over high heat. Add the beans and bay leaves, lower the heat to medium, and simmer the beans until they are very soft, about 2 hours. Skim off the foam that frequently rises to the top of the pot.

2. While the beans are simmering, put the onion, garlic, bell pepper, and cilantro in the bowl of the food processor fitted with the steel blade. Process the vegetables until they are puréed. Add the cumin, coriander, and oregano, pulse two or three times, and set aside at room temperature.

3. When the beans are tender, discard the bay leaves. Add the puréed onion mixture and the tomato purée, stirring and blending the ingredients well. Simmer the soup for another 30 minutes.

4. Purée half the soup, 2 cups at a time, in the food processor fitted with the steel blade. Return the purée to the pot, stir, season with the salt and pepper, and warm over low heat before serving. The soup will have the consistency of both puréed and whole beans.

SERVICE   Ladle the hot soup into soup crocks or bowls. Top each bowl with a dollop of sour cream capped with chopped red onion.

COOK'S TIPS   For a thicker soup, purée additional beans and keep adding them to the soup until it reaches the consistency that pleases you. If the soup is too thick, add vegetable broth to thin it. Other garnishes to serve with the soup are grated cheddar cheese, finely diced tomatoes, and diced yellow, orange, and red bell peppers.

Roasted Bell Peppers Filled with Cheese and Jalapeño Chiles

KITCHENWARE
chef's knife, shallow baking pan large enough to hold 6 half bell peppers in one layer, large skillet, medium bowl

PREPARATION TIME
30 minutes

COOKING TIME
45 minutes

DO-AHEAD
Prepare the onion and jalapeño chiles the day before and store separately, covered, in the refrigerator.

3 large yellow bell peppers
2 tablespoons extra virgin olive oil
1 large onion, diced
2 jalapeño chiles, seeded and finely minced
2 tablespoons minced garlic
⅔ cup diced tomatoes
1 teaspoon salt
1 teaspoon chili powder
2 large eggs, beaten
2 cups ricotta cheese
½ cup fresh bread crumbs
1 cup grated Monterey Jack cheese
Garnish: 2 teaspoons finely chopped fresh flat-leaf parsley

1. Preheat the oven to 350 degrees. Lightly oil the baking pan.

2. Cut the bell peppers in half lengthwise. Carefully remove the seeds, leaving the stem intact to create 6 pepper boats.

3. Heat the oil in the skillet over medium heat and sauté the onion and jalapeño until golden, 8 to 10 minutes. Add the garlic and tomatoes and sauté another 2 minutes. Set the onion mixture aside and cool to room temperature. Season it with the salt and chili powder.

4. Combine the eggs, ricotta, bread crumbs, and half the Monterey Jack in the bowl. Add the cooled onion mixture to the cheese mixture and stuff this into the pepper halves. Arrange the peppers in the baking pan, sprinkle the remaining Monterey Jack over the tops, and bake for 30 minutes.

SERVICE   Sprinkle the top of each pepper with the parsley.

COOK'S TIP   It is fun to mix bell pepper colors. Try a combination of yellow, orange, and red.

Red and White Cabbage Slaw

1 small head white cabbage (about $\frac{1}{2}$ pound)

1 small head red cabbage (about $\frac{1}{2}$ pound)

1 small red onion, finely diced

2 medium grapefruit, peeled, pith removed, sectioned, each section halved crosswise

2 Red Delicious or Gala apples, unpeeled, cored and cut into $\frac{1}{2}$-inch cubes

2 tablespoons finely chopped fresh cilantro, hard stems removed

2 tablespoons rice vinegar

Zest and juice of 1 medium lime

$\frac{1}{2}$ teaspoon ground coriander

$\frac{1}{2}$ teaspoon ground cumin

2 teaspoons honey

6 tablespoons peanut or vegetable oil

Salt and freshly ground pepper

1. Discard the outer leaves of the cabbages and remove the cores. Shred the cabbages in the food processor fitted with the shredding disk or on the large holes of the grater.

2. Toss the cabbage with the onion, grapefruit, apple, and cilantro. Set aside.

3. Whisk the vinegar, lime zest and juice, coriander, cumin, and honey together in the small bowl. Add the oil, stirring constantly until all the ingredients are blended. Season the dressing with salt and pepper to taste, toss it with the cabbage slaw, and blend very well.

4. Allow the cabbage slaw to marinate for 30 minutes at room temperature. Then pour off any liquid that has accumulated and reseason it.

SERVICE Any unusually shaped glass or pottery bowl in your cupboard would be perfect for the slaw.

COOK'S TIP Oranges and pears can be substituted for the apples and grapefruit.

CHAPTER 5

Winter Menus

Winter Fisherman's Chowder

A Hearty Chicken Dinner for a Cold Winter Night

Lamb with the Flavors of India

An Aprés-Ski Pasta Supper

Bold Vegetarian Tastes

It is always fun to share our old family
recipe for Fisherman's Chowder. This one belonged to the matriarch
of our family and was served to us faithfully once a week—on Wednesday.
The chowder tantalizes the taste buds with a rich hearty broth,
root vegetables, and meaty fish.
Mop up the soup with Zucchini and Onion Bread spread with
a thick layer of Sun-Dried Tomato and Dill Butter. If there is such a thing
as a fail-safe bread recipe, this is it. Success on your first try!
The spinach salad, accented with radish and daikon, provides a crisp
contrast to the mellow taste of the chowder.
This is an informal, help-yourself dinner. Use your largest
soup bowls and let your guests fill them to the brim.

Winter Fisherman's Chowder

MENU

HORS D'OEUVRE SUGGESTION
Honey-Glazed Chicken Wings (page 25)

FISHERMAN'S CHOWDER

ZUCCHINI AND ONION BREAD (PAGE 138) WITH SUN-DRIED TOMATO AND DILL BUTTER

SPINACH, RADISH, AND THREADS OF DAIKON WITH VINAIGRETTE

DESSERT SUGGESTION
Citrus Pound Cake with Brandied Raisins (page 262)

WINE SUGGESTION: WHITE
Chardonnay (Mâcon-Villages)

Fisherman's Chowder

KITCHENWARE
chef's knife, peeler, large saucepan, pepper mill

PREPARATION TIME
30 minutes

COOKING TIME
50 minutes

DO-AHEAD
Prepare the chowder through Step 1 the day before, cool to room temperature, and refrigerate it. Complete Step 2 just before serving.

2 tablespoons extra virgin olive oil

1 large yellow onion, diced

2 medium cloves garlic, finely chopped

1 turnip, peeled and cut into $\frac{1}{2}$-inch chunks

1 pound medium new potatoes, quartered

4 large carrots, cut into $\frac{1}{2}$-inch chunks

1 tablespoon tomato paste

1 quart clam juice

1 quart half-and-half

2 bay leaves

1 teaspoon salt

$\frac{1}{2}$ teaspoon freshly ground pepper

2 pounds boned halibut, cut into 2-inch chunks

2 pounds boned cod, cut into 2-inch chunks

Garnish: 2 teaspoons finely chopped fresh chervil or flat-leaf parsley

1. Place the oil in the saucepan over medium heat. Add the onion and sauté for 3 minutes. Add the garlic and sauté 1 minute more. Add the turnip, potatoes, carrots, tomato paste, clam juice, half-and-half, bay leaves, salt, and pepper to the saucepan, stirring well. Bring the chowder to a boil over medium-high heat. Immediately lower the heat to medium-low and gently simmer the chowder, partially covered, for about 30 minutes, or until the vegetables are just resistant to the tines of a fork. Remove and discard the bay leaves.

2. When the vegetables are properly cooked, add the halibut and cod to the saucepan. Continue simmering the chowder for 8 to 10 minutes, until the fish flakes easily when tested with the tines of a fork. Season it again with salt and pepper to taste.

SERVICE Ladle the chowder into 6 deep soup bowls and garnish each serving with the chervil or parsley.

COOK'S TIP Shellfish lovers can add 1 pound of medium shrimp, peeled and deveined, to the chowder during the last 4 minutes of cooking. Reduce the amount of cod and halibut by $\frac{1}{4}$ pound each if the shrimp is added.

Sun-Dried Tomato and Dill Butter

½ pound (2 sticks) unsalted butter, at room temperature
2 small shallots, chopped medium
⅓ cup drained oil-packed sun-dried tomatoes
1 tablespoon finely chopped fresh dill
½ teaspoon salt
¼ teaspoon freshly ground pepper

1. Place the butter, shallots, sun-dried tomatoes, and dill in the bowl of the food processor fitted with the steel blade. Pulse until all the ingredients are blended, scraping down the sides of the bowl often. Season the butter with the salt and pepper.

2. Spoon the butter into the small bowl or crock, cover it well, and refrigerate. Bring it to room temperature before serving.

SERVICE Serve this tasty and colorful butter with the Zucchini and Onion Bread (page 138).

COOK'S TIP Substitute other herbs, such as tarragon, rosemary, or thyme, for the dill and serve the butter with lamb or poultry.

Spinach, Radish, and Threads of Daikon with Vinaigrette

paring knife, large salad bowl, small bowl, whisk

PREPARATION TIME

30 minutes

THE SALAD

1 medium daikon (about ½ pound), trimmed

1 pound baby spinach, trimmed, washed, and dried

12 medium radishes, trimmed and washed, cut into ⅛-inch-thick slices

THE VINAIGRETTE

1 teaspoon chopped garlic

1 tablespoon Dijon mustard

2 tablespoons fresh lemon juice

½ cup extra virgin olive oil

Salt and freshly ground pepper

1. **Make the salad:** Cut the daikon into 3-inch-long julienne strips. Toss the spinach, radishes, and daikon together in the salad bowl.

2. **Make the vinaigrette:** Blend the garlic, mustard, and lemon juice in the small bowl. Slowly whisk in the oil to form an emulsion. Season the vinaigrette with salt and pepper to taste.

SERVICE Toss the vinaigrette with the salad in the salad bowl and serve. You can also serve the salad on 6 individual plates. If you decide to plate the salad, use the daikon as a garnish on top of the mix.

COOK'S TIP Toast ½ cup of slivered almonds and sprinkle them over the salad for added crunch.

Marinating the chicken overnight
in the garlic, fresh rosemary, and white wine creates outstanding flavor.
The pancetta's wonderful smoky flavor and the crunchy herbed potatoes
are a great accompaniment for this or any dinner.
Brussels sprouts coated with nutty brown butter are the perfect vegetable
to complement this menu. To sprout lovers, we promise an even greater
addiction to the little cabbages. To sprout haters, we promise
a newly acquired taste.
A salad of glazed ripe pineapple and Roquefort,
combined with watercress and topped with
walnuts, adds a refreshing touch.

A Hearty Chicken Dinner for a Cold Winter Night

MENU

HORS D'OEUVRE SUGGESTION
Grilled Meatballs with
Indian-Spiced Yogurt Sauce (page 22)

**ROSEMARY CHICKEN AND
PANCETTA BAKED IN WHITE WINE**

HERBED LAYERED POTATOES

**BRUSSELS SPROUTS WITH
BROWN BUTTER AND ORANGE ZEST**

**GLAZED PINEAPPLE, ROQUEFORT CHEESE,
AND WATERCRESS**

DESSERT SUGGESTION
Intensely Moist Triple Chocolate Cake
with Fresh Berries and Cream (page 266)

WINE SUGGESTION: WHITE
Pouilly-Fumé, Sauvignon Blanc

Rosemary Chicken and Pancetta Baked in White Wine

KITCHENWARE

chef's knife, large stainless-steel or glass bowl, food processor, large skillet, slotted spoon, mesh strainer, paper toweling, pepper mill, large oven-to-table baking dish, medium saucepan

PREPARATION TIME

35 minutes

MARINATING TIME

4 hours or overnight

COOKING TIME

40 minutes

DO-AHEAD

Marinate the chicken in the refrigerator overnight. Prepare the shallots for braising 1 day ahead and store them, covered, in the refrigerator.

THE MARINADE

4 medium cloves garlic, minced

1 tablespoon finely chopped fresh rosemary

$\frac{1}{4}$ cup extra virgin olive oil

$\frac{1}{2}$ cup dry white wine

THE CHICKEN

2 roasting chickens (about $3\frac{1}{2}$ pounds each), cut into eighths

$\frac{1}{2}$ pound pancetta

4 large shallots, finely chopped

1 tablespoon extra virgin olive oil (optional)

1 cup dry white wine

1 cup chicken broth, homemade or low-sodium canned

$\frac{1}{2}$ teaspoon freshly ground pepper

4 sprigs fresh rosemary

1. **Make the marinade:** Combine the garlic, rosemary, oil, and wine in the bowl.

2. **Prepare the chicken:** Place the chicken in the marinade, coating each piece thoroughly. Cover the bowl and marinate in the refrigerator for 4 hours or overnight. Bring the chicken to room temperature before continuing the recipe.

3. Preheat the oven to 350 degrees.

4. Place the pancetta in the bowl of the food processor fitted with the steel blade and process until the meat is chopped fine. Sauté the pancetta over medium heat in the skillet until the fat is rendered and the pancetta is lightly crisped, about 10 minutes. Remove the pancetta with a slotted spoon and set it aside.

5. Sauté the shallots over medium heat in the pancetta fat remaining in the skillet until they are translucent, about 3 minutes. Add the shallots to the reserved pancetta.

6. In the same skillet, brown the chicken pieces over medium heat until golden, about 4 minutes on each side. Add the oil to the pan, if needed. *(Strain the fat through a mesh strainer if it collects too many browned pieces, and return it to the pan.)*

7. Once all the chicken has been browned, remove the chicken with a slotted spoon and place on paper toweling. Discard any fat remaining in the skillet. Deglaze the skillet over medium-high heat by adding ½ cup of the wine to the pan and scraping up the browned bits from the bottom.

8. Add the chicken broth, the remaining ½ cup of wine, and the pepper to the skillet, and stir well to combine.

9. Place the chicken in the baking dish and pour the liquid from the skillet around and over it. Place the sprigs of rosemary around the chicken.

10. Bake the chicken for 30 minutes, until it is tender and the juices run clear when the meat is pierced with the tines of a fork.

11. Strain the braising liquid into the saucepan and place it over high heat. Allow the sauce to boil until it is reduced by one-third to one-half the original amount, about 10 minutes. Add the reserved shallots and pancetta.

SERVICE Remove the chicken to a large oval or round serving platter. Mask each piece with some of the sauce and pour the remaining sauce into a sauceboat.

COOK'S TIPS To give an extra dimension to the recipe, add 1 pound of smoky or garlic pork or turkey sausage, sliced on the diagonal into ½-inch-thick pieces, to the casserole before baking.

Herbed Layered Potatoes

KITCHENWARE

chef's knife, medium oven-to-table baking dish, large stockpot, colander, large bowl

PREPARATION TIME

15 minutes

COOKING TIME

45 to 50 minutes

DO-AHEAD

The entire recipe can be prepared early in the day, stored at room temperature, and reheated.

3 tablespoons extra virgin olive oil

3 pounds medium Red Bliss potatoes, unpeeled

4 medium cloves garlic, finely chopped

1 teaspoon finely chopped fresh thyme

1 teaspoon salt

$\frac{1}{2}$ teaspoon freshly ground pepper

Garnish: $\frac{1}{4}$ teaspoon fresh whole thyme leaves

1. Preheat the oven to 400 degrees. Grease the baking dish with 1 tablespoon of the olive oil.

2. Bring 4 quarts of water to a boil over high heat in the stockpot. Reduce the heat, add the potatoes, and simmer over medium heat until they are just resistant to the tines of a fork, about 15 minutes. Drain the potatoes and shock them in cold water to stop the cooking process. Drain the potatoes once more, and slice them into $\frac{1}{4}$-inch-thick rounds.

3. Place the potatoes in the bowl, and toss with the garlic, thyme, salt, pepper, and the remaining 2 tablespoons of oil.

4. Arrange the potatoes in overlapping slices in the baking dish and bake for 25 to 30 minutes, until the potatoes are golden brown and crisp.

SERVICE The potatoes will keep warm in a 250-degree oven for up to 20 minutes. Before serving, sprinkle with the thyme leaves.

COOK'S TIPS If the potatoes are prepared in the morning, they can be reheated in a 325-degree oven. These potatoes also add savory flavor to roasted lamb, beef, or pork.

https://orlandoairport.hyatt.cc

Brussels Sprouts with Brown Butter and Orange Zest

KITCHENWARE

paring knife, zester, steamer basket in a medium saucepan, colander, medium skillet, pepper mill, grater

PREPARATION TIME

30 minutes

COOKING TIME

10 minutes

DO-AHEAD

Clarify the butter and keep it refrigerated in a closed container. Prepare Step 1, and store the sprouts, covered, in the refrigerator. Bring them to room temperature before completing the recipe.

2 pints Brussels sprouts (about 1 ½ pounds), trimmed
6 tablespoons unsalted butter, clarified (see page 285)
2 teaspoons balsamic vinegar
Zest and juice of 1 medium orange
Salt and freshly ground pepper
Garnish: 2 teaspoons finely grated orange zest

1. Score the base of each Brussels sprout and place the sprouts in the steamer basket over boiling water. Steam for 3 to 5 minutes, covered. The Brussels sprouts should be crisp. *(If you do not have a steamer basket, place a small colander filled with the sprouts in the saucepan and steam.)* Drain the sprouts, shock them in cold water to stop the cooking process, and drain again.

2. Heat the butter in the skillet over medium heat until it turns a golden brown. Add the sprouts, tossing constantly to cover each one well with the butter.

3. Turn the heat to high and sprinkle the vinegar, orange zest, and juice over the sprouts. Toss the sprouts until they are well coated and begin to caramelize, about 1 minute. Season them with salt and pepper to taste.

SERVICE The rich brown color created by the combination of caramelized clarified butter and balsamic vinegar shows off the beauty of these vegetables when they are served in an all-white dish. Sprinkle the orange zest garnish over the sprouts before serving.

COOK'S TIP Add ½ pound of diced smoky ham to give an earthy flavor to the glazed sprouts. Add buttered noodles to the menu, double the recipe for the Brussels sprouts, and enjoy a simple late-night supper.

Glazed Pineapple, Roquefort Cheese, and Watercress

KITCHENWARE
chef's knife, zester, small heavy-bottomed saucepan, sharp kitchen knife, nonstick jelly-roll pan, pastry brush

PREPARATION TIME
30 minutes

COOKING TIME
5 minutes

$\frac{1}{2}$ cup packed dark brown sugar

2 teaspoons balsamic vinegar

2 teaspoons minced ginger

Zest and juice of 1 orange

1 ripe pineapple

2 bunches watercress, washed

6 ounces Roquefort cheese, crumbled

$\frac{3}{4}$ cup walnut pieces

1. Combine the sugar, vinegar, ginger, and orange zest and juice in the saucepan over medium heat, and simmer, stirring occasionally, until the sugar has completely dissolved, about 2 minutes. Set the glaze aside while you prepare the salad.

2. Cut off and discard the top of the pineapple. Cut the pineapple in half lengthwise, then into quarters. Loosen the fruit with a knife, cutting between the pineapple meat and the shell. Discard the shell and cut the meat into $\frac{1}{4}$-inch-thick slices. Cut away the core.

3. Preheat the broiler. Set the broiler rack 2 inches from the heating element.

4. Arrange the fruit on the jelly-roll pan, allowing $\frac{1}{2}$ inch between the pieces. Brush the pineapple with half the glaze and broil it for 4 to 5 minutes, until the pieces are golden brown. *(Keep your eyes on the broiler, as sugar burns quickly.)* Cool the pineapple to room temperature. Warm the remaining glaze over low heat and brush the fruit once again.

SERVICE Arrange the watercress in a bed on a round or oval platter. Place the pineapple slices over the watercress. Sprinkle the Roquefort and nuts over the fruit. Drizzle the remaining glaze over the salad.

COOK'S TIP Unpeeled peaches, plums, apples, or pears can be substituted for the pineapple. Vary the fruits according to the season.

This lamb recipe, an invaluable part of my original cooking
school curriculum, is one of my favorites. The yogurt, cumin,
and roasted garlic bring out the rich flavor of the meat. Make a cold lamb
sandwich from the leftovers, slathering on the Pear and Dried Apricot Chutney
for a delicious reminder of a successful dinner.
The cider infuses the green beans with a mild tartness,
as if they were cooked in a bath of wine permeated with apple,
and the flavors of the Indian-Spiced Rice are perfectly matched
to the yogurt and cumin in the lamb recipe.
Complete the menu with a hearty Spinach Bread, the epitome
of comfort food, and don't hesitate to top the still-warm bread
with a slice of your favorite cheese.

Lamb with the Flavors of India

MENU

**HORS D'OEUVRE
SUGGESTION**
Salt-Cured Cilantro-Rubbed Salmon on
Cilantro Crostini with Balsamic–Roasted
Garlic Aioli Sauce (page 35)

**LAMB BRAISED WITH
CUMIN, YOGURT, AND GARLIC**

PEAR AND DRIED APRICOT CHUTNEY

INDIAN-SPICED RICE AND CHERRY TOMATOES

CRUNCHY GREEN BEANS SOAKED IN CIDER

SPINACH BREAD

DESSERT SUGGESTION
Creamy Cheesecake with Orange and Chocolate (page 264)

WINE SUGGESTION: RED
Côtes du Rhône, Red Zinfandel

Lamb Braised with Cumin, Yogurt, and Garlic

KITCHENWARE

chef's knife, pepper mill, medium stainless-steel or noncorrosive bowl, plastic wrap, 2 large bowls, colander, paper toweling, medium oven-to-table baking pan, wooden spoon

PREPARATION TIME

40 minutes

MARINATING TIME

4 to 24 hours

COOKING TIME

1½ hours

DO-AHEAD

Prepare the lamb and combine it with the marinade the day before.

Two 8-ounce containers yogurt

6 large cloves garlic, minced

1 tablespoon ground cumin

1 teaspoon salt

¼ teaspoon freshly ground pepper

4 pounds boneless, well-trimmed leg of lamb, cut into 1-inch cubes

1 cup all-purpose flour

¼ cup plus 2 tablespoons extra virgin olive oil

1 large Spanish onion, finely chopped

1 cup dry red wine

3 cups chicken broth, homemade or low-sodium canned

2 pounds fresh ripe tomatoes, peeled and finely chopped

¼ cup finely chopped fresh cilantro

2 large heads roasted garlic (see page 286)

1. Combine 1 container (8 ounces) of the yogurt with the minced garlic, cumin, salt, and pepper in the medium bowl. Blend well and add the lamb, coating each piece with the marinade. Toss well, cover with plastic wrap, and place in the refrigerator for 4 hours or overnight.

2. Preheat the oven to 350 degrees.

3. Place the flour in a large bowl. Drain the lamb in the colander, discarding the marinade. Pat the lamb dry with paper toweling and toss it with the flour, coating each piece well.

4. Heat ¼ cup of the oil in the baking pan over medium heat. Sauté the lamb in small batches until it is a rich golden brown, about 5 minutes. (Do not overcrowd the pan.) Transfer the lamb to the other large bowl with the browned bits that have accumulated in the pan.

5. Add the remaining 2 tablespoons oil to the baking pan and sauté the onion over medium heat until translucent, about 3 minutes. Add the wine and then the chicken stock. With a wooden spoon, scrape up any bits remaining on the bottom of the pan. Add the tomatoes, 2 tablespoons of the cilantro, and the lamb. Stir well. Cover the baking pan and braise the lamb in the oven about 1½ hours, until it is tender.

6. Stir the roasted garlic paste and the remaining 2 teaspoons of cilantro into the baking pan during the last 10 minutes of cooking to blend the flavors. Season the lamb with additional salt and pepper to taste.

SERVICE It is fun to serve the lamb in large soup plates. Don't forget to pass the Pear and Dried Apricot Chutney.

COOK'S TIP Add 2 pounds of trimmed and blanched green beans to the lamb during the last 30 minutes of cooking.

Pear and Dried Apricot Chutney

KITCHENWARE
**chef's knife, zester, small
saucepan**

PREPARATION
TIME
20 minutes

COOKING TIME
25 minutes

DO-AHEAD
**Prepare the chutney up to 4
days ahead, cover, and
refrigerate it. Bring it back to
room temperature before
serving.**

1 ½ cups pear nectar

¾ cup packed dark brown sugar

2 pounds Bosc or Anjou pears, peeled, cored,
    and cut in ¼-inch dice

8 ounces dried apricots, chopped medium

2 ounces dried currants

1 teaspoon minced ginger

½ teaspoon ground cumin

½ cup cider vinegar

1 tablespoon lemon zest

¼ cup fresh lemon juice

1. Bring the pear nectar to a simmer over medium-high heat in the saucepan. Stir in the brown sugar and simmer until the sugar has completely dissolved, about 2 minutes.

2. Combine the pears, apricots, currants, ginger, cumin, vinegar, and lemon zest and juice with the pear nectar. Reduce the heat to medium and simmer the fruit, partially covered, stirring occasionally, until the chutney has thickened but remains slightly chunky, 20 to 25 minutes. Remove it from the heat and cool to room temperature.

SERVICE Spoon the chutney into a serving bowl and serve with the braised lamb.

COOK'S TIP There are so many dried fruits available today. Substitute dried apples for the pears or apricots. It's fun to play with different fruit mixes for this dish.

Indian-Spiced Rice and Cherry Tomatoes

KITCHENWARE

chef's knife, medium saucepan,
wooden spoon, pepper mill,
strainer, medium skillet

PREPARATION
TIME
10 minutes

COOKING TIME
30 minutes

DO-AHEAD
Prepare the onion, garlic, and
tomatoes. Juice the lemons.
Store each one separately,
covered, in the refrigerator,
up to one day ahead.

$\frac{1}{4}$ cup plus 2 tablespoons extra virgin olive oil

1 medium red onion, finely chopped

2 large cloves garlic, minced

2 cups basmati rice, rinsed and drained

$\frac{1}{2}$ teaspoon ground turmeric

$\frac{1}{2}$ teaspoon ground cardamom

$\frac{1}{4}$ teaspoon freshly ground pepper

3 cups chicken broth, homemade or low-sodium canned

$\frac{1}{2}$ cup dry white wine

$\frac{1}{4}$ cup fresh lemon juice

18 small to medium cherry tomatoes, stemmed, washed,
   and halved

Salt

Garnish: $\frac{1}{4}$ teaspoon finely chopped fresh flat-leaf parsley

1. Heat $\frac{1}{4}$ cup of the oil over medium heat in the saucepan.
   Add the onion and sauté, stirring with a wooden spoon,
   until it is soft and translucent, 2 to 3 minutes. Add the
   garlic and sauté 1 minute more. Add the rice, turmeric,
   cardamom, and pepper, and sauté, stirring constantly,
   until each grain of rice is transparent and well coated
   with the spices, about 1 minute.

2. Add the broth, wine, and lemon juice and bring the liquid to a brisk simmer over high heat. Lower the heat and gently simmer the rice, covered, for 12 to 15 minutes, until the liquid has been absorbed. Let it stand, covered, for 10 minutes.

3. While the rice is cooking, place the remaining 2 tablespoons oil in the skillet and sauté the tomatoes, stirring often, until they have just wilted and are heated through, 2 minutes. Drain off the excess liquid.

SERVICE   Gently blend the tomatoes with the rice and season the mixture with salt and additional pepper to taste. Spoon the rice into a colorful 2- to 3-inch-deep oval or round serving dish. Fluff the rice with a fork and scatter the parsley over the top.

COOK'S TIP   You can make the rice early in the day and store, covered, at room temperature. Reheat it in a 325-degree oven until hot. Do not add the tomatoes until just before the rice is reheated.

Crunchy Green Beans Soaked in Cider

KITCHENWARE

paring knife, grater, heavy-bottomed medium saucepan, slotted spoon, 2 large bowls, whisk, pepper mill

PREPARATION TIME

20 minutes

COOKING TIME

4 minutes

DO-AHEAD

The beans can be blanched several hours in advance of serving and stored at room temperature.

1 ½ pounds young green beans, stemmed

2 cups apple cider

2 Red or Golden Delicious apples, unpeeled, cored, halved, and cut into 1-inch dice

2 tablespoons extra virgin olive oil

1 teaspoon cider vinegar

½ teaspoon grated ginger

1 teaspoon salt

½ teaspoon freshly ground pepper

Garnish: ½ teaspoon grated ginger

1. Blanch the green beans (see page 284).

2. Bring the cider to a boil over high heat in the saucepan. Lower the heat to medium, add the apples, and simmer for 4 minutes. Remove the apples with a slotted spoon and set them aside in a bowl.

3. Whisk the warm cider with the oil, cider vinegar, and ½ teaspoon ginger in the other bowl. Add the beans and apples, stirring until they are well coated with the dressing. Season with the salt and pepper.

SERVICE Sprinkle ½ teaspoon ginger over the beans and serve them at room temperature. A bright red or yellow dish will show off the brilliant green of the beans.

COOK'S TIPS The beans travel very well and are great for picnics or tailgate parties. Crisp crumbled bacon, leftover diced baked ham, and pecans are all enhancements that work wonderfully with the beans.

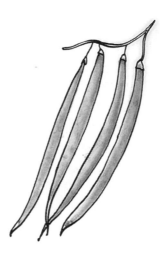

Spinach Bread

KITCHENWARE

chef's knife, greased 9-inch
round cake pan, 2 large bowls,
large skillet, kitchen towel or
plastic wrap, rack

PREPARATION
TIME

30 minutes plus 1½ hours
rising time

COOKING TIME
45 minutes

DO-AHEAD

Prepare the leeks up to 1 day
ahead and store them,
covered, in the refrigerator.

1 tablespoon active dry yeast

4 tablespoons extra virgin olive oil

3 medium leeks, white part only, washed and finely chopped

1½ pounds fresh spinach, washed, stemmed, and finely chopped, or one 10-ounce box chopped frozen spinach, defrosted and squeezed dry

1 teaspoon finely chopped fresh sage

⅛ teaspoon cayenne

½ teaspoon salt

2 tablespoons sugar

3 to 4 cups all-purpose flour

1. Dissolve the yeast in 1 cup warm water in a bowl.

2. Heat 2 tablespoons of the oil in the skillet over medium heat and sauté the leeks until they soften, about 3 minutes. Add the spinach and cook, stirring constantly, until the spinach has completely wilted, 1 to 2 minutes. Season the vegetables with the sage, cayenne, and salt. Set aside and cool for 10 minutes.

3. Mix the spinach, sugar, remaining 2 tablespoons oil, and 3 cups of the flour with the yeast. Using your hands, blend the ingredients well until the dough leaves the sides of the bowl. Turn the dough onto a floured work surface and knead it, adding more flour if necessary, until it is soft, 4 to 5 minutes. Put the dough into a lightly greased bowl, cover the bowl with a damp kitchen towel or plastic wrap, and let it rise until doubled in size, about 1 hour.

4. Punch the dough down and knead it on a board for three to four turns. Shape it into a ball and press it into the prepared cake pan. Cover the pan lightly with a damp kitchen towel or plastic wrap and let the dough rise about 30 minutes.

5. Preheat the oven to 425 degrees.

6. Bake the bread for 10 minutes. Lower the heat to 350 degrees and bake 30 minutes more. Cool the bread for 5 minutes in the pan, then invert it onto a cake rack.

SERVICE   The bread should be served warm. Slice the loaf with a serrated knife, line a basket with a white napkin, and set the sliced bread in the basket, covered with the corners of the napkin to keep it warm.

COOK'S TIP   Add ½ cup of finely grated Asiago cheese to the spinach mixture to give extra richness to the bread.

This is a great meal to look forward to
after an exhausting day on the slopes or a good workout at the gym.
The flavors in the Pasta Sausage Spirals intensify when teamed with the Cheesy
Tomato Sauce and the garlic and lemon in the broccoli rabe.
Focaccia, a most enjoyable culinary treat, can be made complex
with the addition of many ingredients—like a pizza with seven toppings—
or it can be simple yet intense in flavor. A topping of two cheeses,
scallions, and kosher salt is definitely uncomplicated. This focaccia
adds the crispness needed to round out the menu and deserves
many repeat performances.
The whole menu can be prepared the day before and finished
just before your guests arrive—or let them help you put
on the finishing touches in the kitchen.

An Après-Ski Pasta Supper

MENU

HORS D'OEUVRE SUGGESTION
Garlicky Doused Shrimp (page 13)

**PASTA SAUSAGE SPIRALS
WITH CHEESY TOMATO SAUCE**

**GARLIC LOVERS'
BROCCOLI RABE WITH LEMON**

**GREEN ONION DOUBLE-CHEESE
HERBED FOCACCIA**

DESSERT SUGGESTION
Chocolate Chocolate Chip Banana Ice Cream Cake
with Pecan Rum Caramel Sauce (page 257)

WINE SUGGESTION: WHITE
Sauvignon Blanc, Pinot Grigio

Pasta Sausage Spirals with Cheesy Tomato Sauce

KITCHENWARE

chef's knife, grater, large
skillet, slotted spoon, large
bowl, pepper mill, large
saucepan, 12 x 22-inch piece of
aluminum foil, pastry brush,
large lasagna pan, serrated
knife

PREPARATION
TIME
40 minutes

COOKING TIME
40 minutes

DO-AHEAD
The spirals can be assembled
several hours ahead and
refrigerated.

1 ½ pounds ground pork or turkey sausage meat

1 large onion, finely chopped

2 cloves garlic, finely chopped

1 tablespoon crushed fennel seeds

¾ teaspoon table salt

½ teaspoon freshly ground pepper

2 tablespoons finely chopped fresh basil

1 large bunch arugula, washed, stemmed, and finely chopped

1 cup freshly grated Parmesan cheese

½ pound coarsely grated mozzarella cheese

3 large eggs, beaten

2 tablespoons kosher salt

½ pound dried lasagna noodles (6 unbroken noodles)

2 teaspoons extra virgin olive oil

1 recipe Cheesy Tomato Sauce (recipe follows)

1. **Make the filling:** Sauté the sausage in the skillet over medium heat until it is golden brown and no pink remains. Remove the sausage with a slotted spoon and transfer it to the bowl. Reserve the drippings in the pan.

2. Reheat the sausage drippings and sauté the onion over medium heat for 3 minutes. Add the garlic and cook 1 minute more. Combine the onion mixture, fennel seeds, table salt, pepper, basil, arugula, Parmesan, mozzarella, and eggs with the sausage, blending all the ingredients well.

3. **Cook the pasta:** Fill the saucepan with cold water. Add the kosher salt, cover the pan, and bring the water to a rolling boil over high heat. Add the noodles, stir well a few times to prevent the pasta from sticking, and cook, uncovered, over medium-high heat until just tender, 8 to 10 minutes, or according to package directions. Do not overcook. *(The lasagna will not fit into the pot at first because the noodles are quite long. They will become pliable and can easily be pressed down into the cooking water with a wooden spoon after 1 to 2 minutes of cooking.)* Drain the noodles.

4. While the pasta is cooking, brush the aluminum foil lightly with 1 teaspoon of the olive oil. Lay the lasagna noodles in single strips on the foil. Cover the noodles with the foil and set aside at room temperature.

5. Assemble the spirals: Preheat the oven to 350 degrees. Lightly brush the lasagna pan with the remaining teaspoon of oil.

6. Spread a thin layer of Cheesy Tomato Sauce, about $1\frac{1}{2}$ cups, on the bottom of the pan.

7. On a clean work surface, lay the noodles with the short end of the pasta facing you. Spread 3 tablespoons of the sausage filling over each noodle, leaving about 2 inches at the top of the noodle without filling.

8. Tightly roll the noodle into a cylinder, rolling away from you until you reach the end. If any filling falls out as you roll, stuff it back into the spiral. Cut each spiral into 2 pieces with a serrated knife.

9. Place the pasta spirals flat in the baking dish, cut side up. Do not overcrowd the pan. Cover the spirals with about 3 cups of the Cheesy Tomato Sauce and bake them for 40 minutes, until piping hot.

SERVICE   Serve two spirals to each guest.

COOK'S TIP   If you refrigerate the formed spirals for 2 hours before slicing, the pasta will be easier to slice.

Cheesy Tomato Sauce

KITCHENWARE
chef's knife, grater, large
saucepan, pepper mill, food
processor

**PREPARATION
TIME**
15 minutes

COOKING TIME
40 minutes

DO-AHEAD
The sauce can be made up to
1 week in advance and
refrigerated, tightly covered.

3 tablespoons extra virgin olive oil

1 large onion, finely chopped

3 medium cloves garlic, finely chopped

Two 28-ounce cans Italian-style peeled plum tomatoes
with their juice

1 pound fresh plum tomatoes, seeded and coarsely chopped

2 tablespoons coarsely chopped fresh basil, tough
stems removed

1 cup dry red wine

1 teaspoon salt

½ teaspoon freshly ground pepper

1 cup finely grated Parmesan cheese

1. Heat the oil over medium heat in the saucepan and sauté the onion until softened, 3 to 4 minutes. Add the garlic and sauté 1 minute more.

2. Add the canned tomatoes, fresh tomatoes, basil, wine, salt, and pepper and simmer the sauce, uncovered, over medium-low heat for 30 minutes. Add the cheese and simmer 5 minutes more.

3. Pour the sauce, in batches, into the bowl of the food processor fitted with the steel blade and process until smooth, about 30 seconds. Return the sauce to the saucepan and season it to taste with additional salt and pepper. Reheat before serving.

COOK'S TIPS This is a great sauce for any of your favorite pastas. It can be frozen for up to 3 months. Reseason the sauce after refrigerating or freezing.

Garlic Lovers' Broccoli Rabe with Lemon

KITCHENWARE
paring knife, large saucepan, colander, large skillet, pepper mill, zester

PREPARATION
TIME
15 minutes

COOKING TIME
7 minutes

DO-AHEAD
The recipe can be prepared through Step 2 several hours ahead and stored, covered, in the refrigerator. Finish Step 3 just before serving.

2 pounds broccoli rabe

1 tablespoon plus 1 teaspoon salt

3 tablespoons extra virgin olive oil

3 large cloves garlic, finely chopped

3 large roasted cloves garlic, mashed (see page 286)

$\frac{1}{4}$ cup fresh lemon juice

$\frac{1}{2}$ teaspoon freshly ground pepper

Garnish: 1 teaspoon finely grated lemon zest

1. Cut off and discard the bruised leaves from the broccoli rabe stems. Cut each stem into 1$\frac{1}{2}$-inch diagonal pieces.

2. Bring 6 quarts of water to a boil over high heat in the saucepan. Add 1 tablespoon of the salt and the broccoli rabe. Lower the heat to medium and simmer, uncovered, until just tender but still crisp to the bite, 3 to 4 minutes. Drain the broccoli rabe, shock it in cold water, and drain it well again. Set it aside.

3. While the broccoli rabe is cooking, heat the oil in the skillet over medium heat and sauté the chopped garlic for 30 seconds. Raise the heat to high and add the broccoli rabe, roasted garlic, and lemon juice. Stir briskly until all the ingredients are well incorporated. Season the dish with the remaining 1 teaspoon salt and the pepper.

SERVICE The bright green color of the broccoli rabe stands out when served from a white or black crockery dish. Sprinkle the top with lemon zest just before serving.

COOK'S TIP For a burst of color, add 1 red or yellow bell pepper, seeded and medium chopped, to the broccoli rabe in Step 3.

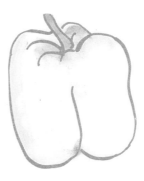

Green Onion Double-Cheese Herbed Focaccia

KITCHENWARE

chef's knife, 9 x 12-inch baking sheet with 1-inch sides (if unavailable, use a 2-inch-deep rectangular cake pan), grater, medium bowl, large bowl, damp kitchen towel or plastic wrap

PREPARATION TIME

30 minutes plus 1½ hours rising time

COOKING TIME

20 minutes

DO-AHEAD

Prepare the scallions and grate the cheeses up to 1 day ahead and store them separately, covered, in the refrigerator.

4 tablespoons extra virgin olive oil

1 package active dry yeast

4 scallions, white and some green part, trimmed and sliced into ⅛-inch-thick rounds

2 ounces Asiago cheese, grated

½ cup freshly grated Parmesan cheese

1 tablespoon finely chopped fresh basil

2¾ to 3¼ cups all-purpose flour

1 teaspoon table salt

½ tablespoon kosher or sea salt

Garnish: 4 sprigs fresh basil

1. Grease the baking sheet with 1 tablespoon of the oil.

2. Place 1 cup warm water in the medium bowl. Sprinkle the yeast over the water, blend, and let stand for 10 minutes.

3. Add the remaining 3 tablespoons oil, the scallions, Asiago, ¼ cup of the Parmesan, and the chopped basil to the yeast and blend well. Add 2¾ cups of the flour and the table salt. Stir the mixture until the dough forms a soft sticky ball.

4. Transfer the dough to a lightly floured surface and knead it, adding the remaining flour as necessary, to form a shiny elastic ball, about 10 minutes.

5. Turn the dough into a large lightly oiled bowl. Rotate the dough once to coat all sides with oil. Cover the bowl with a damp kitchen towel or plastic wrap and let the dough rise at room temperature for 1 hour.

6. Preheat the oven to 450 degrees.

7. Press and stretch the dough to fit into the baking sheet and let it rise 25 minutes, covered lightly with the towel or plastic wrap. Sprinkle the Kosher salt over the top of the focaccia and bake it for 20 to 25 minutes, until it is a toasty brown. Scatter the remaining $\frac{1}{4}$ cup Parmesan over the focaccia while it is still piping hot. Let it cool for 15 minutes at room temperature before serving.

SERVICE   Cut the focaccia into 2 x 3-inch rectangles or pie-shaped wedges. Arrange it in a flat basket and garnish it with the sprigs of fresh basil.

COOK'S TIP   Mix $\frac{1}{2}$ cup of diced plum tomatoes with 2 tablespoons of olive oil and spread over the top of the focaccia before it is baked.

Thinly sliced, baked eggplant provides
the surprising "wrapper" for a tangy gratin filling.
The well-seasoned marriage of Swiss chard
and spinach makes the perfect partner for the wrap,
while the gentle bite of jicama joins mango and orange in a
unique and refreshing salad that is perfectly dressed for the
occasion in an Orange Cilantro Vinaigrette.
The menu would not be complete without our special corn bread.
During an annual conference of Les Dames d'Escoffier International
in Atlanta, Georgia, we were introduced to White Lily Flour, whose
magic creates incredibly light bread, rolls, and pastries. Of course,
you can use your favorite self-rising flour
to make this satisfying bread.

Bold Vegetarian Tastes

MENU

HORS D'OEUVRE SUGGESTION
Gorgonzola and Caramelized Onion Tart (page 16)

**EGGPLANT, ASIAGO, AND QUINOA
WRAP WITH HOT TOMATO SALSA**

SPINACH, CHARD, LEEKS, AND LEMON

MONTEREY JACK CORN BREAD

**JICAMA, MANGO, AND WALNUT SALAD
WITH ORANGE CILANTRO VINAIGRETTE**

DESSERT SUGGESTION
Cheddar Cheese Crusted Apple Pie (page 254)

WINE SUGGESTION: RED
Merlot, Pinot Noir

Eggplant, Asiago, and Quinoa Wrap with Hot Tomato Salsa

KITCHENWARE
chef's knife, peeler, grater, pastry brush, large shallow baking dish, fine-mesh strainer, small saucepan, 2 baking sheets, large skillet, pepper mill, paper toweling

PREPARATION TIME
1 hour

COOKING TIME
30 minutes

DO-AHEAD
Prepare the recipe through Step 5 up to 1 day ahead and store the eggplant and filling separately, covered, in the refrigerator.

4 $\frac{1}{2}$ tablespoons extra virgin olive oil

1 cup quinoa (see Note)

2 cups vegetable broth, canned or Morga cubes (see Note)

3 large eggplants (about $\frac{3}{4}$ pound each), ends removed

6 scallions, white and green parts, cut into $\frac{1}{8}$-inch-thick rounds

2 large carrots, trimmed, peeled, cut into $\frac{1}{4}$-inch dice

2 medium cloves garlic, finely chopped

1 jalapeño chile, seeded and finely chopped

2 tablespoons finely chopped fresh cilantro

2 tablespoons rice vinegar

1 $\frac{1}{2}$ cups grated Asiago cheese

1 cup yogurt

$\frac{1}{2}$ teaspoon salt

$\frac{1}{4}$ teaspoon freshly ground pepper

1 recipe Hot Tomato Salsa (recipe follows)

Garnish: 2 teaspoons finely chopped fresh cilantro

1. Preheat the oven to 350 degrees. Brush the baking dish with $\frac{1}{2}$ tablespoon of the oil.

2. Place the quinoa in the strainer and rinse it thoroughly under cold running water for 30 seconds. Shake the strainer to remove any clinging water.

3. Place the quinoa and broth in the saucepan, cover, and bring the liquid to a boil over medium-high heat. Immediately reduce the heat and cook the quinoa, covered, for 15 minutes, until all the liquid is absorbed and the kernels are transparent. Uncover the pan and set it aside.

4. While the quinoa is cooking, brush the baking sheets with 1 tablespoon of the oil. Cut the eggplants lengthwise into $\frac{1}{4}$-inch-thick slices (about 18 slices) and arrange them on the baking sheets. Brush the top side of the eggplant slices with 1 tablespoon of oil and bake about 15 minutes, until they are pliable. Remove the eggplant from the oven and set it aside at room temperature.

5. Heat the remaining 2 tablespoons of oil in the skillet over medium heat and sauté the scallions for 2 minutes. Add the carrots and continue to sauté for 4 minutes. Add the garlic and cook 1 minute more. Blend the jalapeño, 2 tablespoons cilantro, rice vinegar, $\frac{3}{4}$ cup of the Asiago, and the yogurt with the vegetables. Combine the vegetables with the quinoa, stir well, and season with the salt and pepper.

6. Spread $\frac{1}{4}$ cup of quinoa filling over each eggplant slice and roll it from the wide end to form a bundle. Cover the bottom of the prepared baking dish with about 1 cup of the Hot Tomato Salsa. Arrange the eggplant bundles, seam side down, over the salsa, spoon another 1 cup of salsa over the top, and sprinkle with the remaining $\frac{3}{4}$ cup Asiago. Bake 30 minutes, until the sauce is bubbly and the cheese is lightly browned.

SERVICE Sprinkle the top of the eggplant wraps with the cilantro garnish and serve them directly from the baking dish. You should have two per person, with leftovers for heartier appetites. With paper toweling saturated with warm water and squeezed dry, wipe any excess browned cheese and sauce that might have formed on the inside of the baking dish during the baking.

COOK'S TIPS Adding a second jalapeño will make your mouth tingle. Taste the finished quinoa filling to judge just how much of the hot to add.

Note: Quinoa (a grain) and Morga cubes are available in natural food stores and some supermarkets.

Hot Tomato Salsa

KITCHENWARE
chef's knife, medium saucepan,
pepper mill

**PREPARATION
TIME**
20 minutes

COOKING TIME
30 minutes

DO-AHEAD
Prepare the salsa up to 4 days
ahead and store it, covered, in
the refrigerator.

2 tablespoons extra virgin olive oil

8 scallions, trimmed and finely chopped

4 large cloves garlic, finely chopped

Two 28-ounce cans diced tomatoes with their juice

4 small serrano or jalapeño chiles, seeded and finely
chopped

$\frac{1}{4}$ cup red wine vinegar

6 tablespoons fresh lime juice

$\frac{1}{4}$ cup tequila

2 teaspoons finely chopped fresh cilantro

$\frac{1}{2}$ teaspoon salt

$\frac{1}{4}$ teaspoon freshly ground pepper

1. Heat the oil in the saucepan over medium heat. Add the
   scallions and sauté for 3 minutes. Add the garlic and
   sauté 1 minute more.

2. Stir the tomatoes, serranos, vinegar, lime juice, tequila,
   and cilantro into the saucepan and cook uncovered over
   medium heat for 25 minutes. Season it with the salt and
   pepper. The sauce is chunky, not smooth.

COOK'S TIPS The Hot Tomato Salsa is perfect as a taco
dip. Think of making it whenever you are serving tortillas or
enchiladas.

Spinach, Chard, Leeks, and Lemon

KITCHENWARE

chef's knife, large skillet, pepper mill

PREPARATION TIME

30 minutes

COOKING TIME

15 to 20 minutes

3 tablespoons extra virgin olive oil

3 medium leeks, white part only, trimmed and washed, halved lengthwise, and thinly sliced

2 medium cloves garlic, finely chopped

1½ pounds red Swiss chard, stemmed, washed, and coarsely chopped

1½ pounds baby spinach, stemmed and washed

½ teaspoon ground cumin

½ teaspoon salt

¼ teaspoon freshly ground pepper

2 tablespoons fresh lemon juice

Garnish: Pinch of cayenne

1. Heat 2 tablespoons of the oil in the skillet over medium-high heat. Add the leeks and sauté for 5 minutes. Add the garlic and sauté 1 minute more. Mix the chard with the leeks and continue to cook, stirring often, until the chard wilts, 4 to 5 minutes. Add the remaining oil and the spinach, stirring the vegetables together until the spinach has wilted, 1 to 2 minutes.

2. Blend the cumin, salt, and pepper with the vegetables in the skillet. If serving at once, add the lemon juice now. If serving later, add the lemon juice to the vegetables just before serving. Toss well and reseason to taste with additional salt and pepper.

SERVICE Transfer the spinach and chard to a colorful crockery bowl, sprinkle with the cayenne, and serve immediately.

COOK'S TIP Serve the spinach and chard over steamed basmati rice for a heartier dish.

Monterey Jack Corn Bread

KITCHENWARE
chef's knife, grater,
8-inch round cake pan,
medium bowl, large bowl

PREPARATION TIME
20 minutes

COOKING TIME
25 minutes

DO-AHEAD
Chop the chiles and grate the cheese up to 1 day ahead and store them separately, covered, in the refrigerator.

2 teaspoons vegetable shortening
1 ¼ cups self-rising flour
1 cup white cornmeal
2 teaspoons baking powder
2 tablespoons sugar
1 teaspoon salt
½ teaspoon chili powder
2 large eggs, lightly beaten
1 cup buttermilk
2 medium jalapeño chiles, seeded and finely chopped
1 cup finely grated Monterey Jack cheese

1. Preheat the oven to 425 degrees. Grease the pan with the shortening.

2. Place the flour, cornmeal, baking powder, sugar, salt, and chili powder in the medium bowl and mix well.

3. Combine the eggs, buttermilk, jalapeños, and Monterey Jack in the large bowl. Add the dry ingredients and stir until well moistened. (Do not overblend; ignore the lumps that may remain.)

4. Pour the batter into the prepared pan and bake for 20 to 25 minutes. The corn bread is ready when the top is golden and a toothpick inserted in the center comes out clean.

SERVICE This light, moist bread should be served warm. Gild the lily by placing a crock of whipped butter on the table.

COOK'S TIP For an extra burst of hot, use Monterey Jack that's flavored with jalapeño.

Jicama, Mango, and Walnut Salad with Orange Cilantro Vinaigrette

KITCHENWARE

chef's knife, pepper mill, salad
bowl

PREPARATION
TIME

30 minutes

DO-AHEAD

The fruit and vinaigrette can
be prepared a few hours
before serving.

6 navel oranges or tangelos, peeled, white pith removed, and
sectioned

1 jicama (about 1 pound), peeled and cut into julienne strips

2 mangoes, peeled, seeded, and cut into medium dice

½ cup walnut pieces

2 teaspoons fresh lime juice

Salt and freshly ground pepper to taste

1 recipe Orange Cilantro Vinaigrette (recipe follows)

1. Combine all the ingredients except the Orange Cilantro
Vinaigrette in a salad bowl.

SERVICE Toss the salad with the Orange Cilantro
Vinaigrette 15 minutes before serving.

COOK'S TIP Substitute other fruits, such as winter mel-
ons or pears, for the oranges or mangoes.

Orange Cilantro Vinaigrette

KITCHENWARE

chef's knife, small bowl, whisk, pepper mill

PREPARATION
TIME

5 minutes

1 small shallot, finely chopped

2 tablespoons fresh orange juice

2 tablespoons white wine vinegar

2 tablespoons washed finely chopped stemmed
    fresh cilantro

5 tablespoons extra virgin olive oil

Salt and freshly ground pepper

1. Combine the shallot, orange juice, vinegar, and cilantro in
   the small bowl and blend well. Whisk the oil into the
   bowl until all the ingredients are well blended. Season
   the vinaigrette with salt and pepper to taste.

Desserts for All Seasons

Blackberry Brandy Fresh Plum Bread Pudding

KITCHENWARE

sharp knife, melon baller, large bowl, small bowl, electric mixer, small rectangular oven-to-table baking dish, plastic wrap, two 1-pound cans, large roasting pan

PREPARATION TIME

30 minutes

SETTING TIME

15 minutes

BAKING TIME

45 minutes

DO-AHEAD:

Make the pudding early in the day and reheat it in a water bath in a 300-degree oven for 20 to 25 minutes. If the pudding is made the day before and refrigerated, bring it to room temperature before reheating.

2 pounds firm but ripe medium red, black, or purple plums

4 tablespoons blackberry brandy

7 ounces miniature dried fruit pieces, such as Sun-Maid Fruit Bits

8 large eggs

1 quart heavy cream

1 $\frac{1}{2}$ cups sugar

2 teaspoons ground cinnamon

1 teaspoon ground allspice

2 tablespoons pure vanilla extract

Zest and juice of 1 small orange

1 loaf day-old challah bread or baguette, with crust, cut into $\frac{3}{4}$-inch cubes

1. Preheat the oven to 350 degrees.

2. Cut the plums in half lengthwise. *(The knife will tap the pit in the center as you slice.)* Twist the plum halves in opposite directions to separate them from the pit. With the large end of a melon baller, remove the pit. Cut each plum half into quarters and cut each quarter into $\frac{1}{8}$-inch-thick slices. Put the plums in the large bowl and toss with 2 tablespoons of the brandy.

3. Place the dried fruit in the small bowl and toss with the remaining 2 tablespoons of brandy.

4. Combine the eggs and cream in the large bowl of the electric mixer fitted with the whisk attachment. Beat on medium speed until well blended, about 2 minutes. Add the sugar and beat for 1 minute more. Add the cinnamon, allspice, vanilla, and orange zest and juice and beat for 30 seconds more.

5. Cover the bottom of the baking dish evenly with the bread cubes. Cover the cubes evenly with the plums and their juices. Whisk the custard well and pour it over the plums. Scatter the dried fruit and the soaking brandy over the plums. Cover the top of the baking dish with plastic wrap and weight it with the 1-pound cans for 15 minutes.

6. Fill the roasting pan with 2 inches of warm water. Remove the weights and plastic wrap from the baking dish and set the dish into the water bath in the roasting pan. Bake the bread pudding for 45 minutes, until a cake tester or knife inserted in the center comes out clean.

SERVICE   Remove the baking dish from the roasting pan and let it stand at room temperature for 15 minutes. To experience all the wonderful flavors in the bread pudding, serve it warm.

COOK'S TIP   Nectarines can be substituted for the plums.

Cheddar Cheese Crusted Apple Pie

KITCHENWARE

grater, food processor, plastic wrap, apple corer, sharp knife, large bowl, rolling pin, 10-inch pie pan, scissors, small knife, pastry brush, aluminum foil, rack

PREPARATION TIME

30 minutes

BAKING TIME

45 minutes

THE CRUST

⅔ cup unsalted butter

2 cups all-purpose flour

2 tablespoons granulated sugar

½ teaspoon salt

½ cup finely grated sharp cheddar cheese

THE PIE

5 large Golden Delicious or Granny Smith apples
   (about 2 pounds)

1 tablespoon fresh lemon juice

1 cup plus 1 tablespoon Brownulated sugar

1 teaspoon ground mace

2 teaspoons ground cinnamon

3 tablespoons unsalted butter

Egg wash (see page 285)

1. **Make the crust:** Break ⅔ cup of butter into 1-inch pieces. Place the flour, granulated sugar, salt, and butter into the bowl of the food processor fitted with the steel blade and pulse until the mixture resembles coarse meal. Add the cheddar and pulse three times more to incorporate the cheese into the dough. Add 6 tablespoons of cold water and pulse until the dough has come together into a smooth ball, about twice more. If the dough is dry, add 1 more tablespoon of cold water.

2. Remove the dough and cut it in half. Form each half into a disk and wrap in plastic wrap. Refrigerate the dough while making the pie filling.

3. **Make the pie filling:** Preheat the oven to 375 degrees.

4. Cut the apples with an apple corer into wedges. Slice each wedge of apple into 3 pieces. You should have about 10 cups. Place the apple slices in the large bowl and toss them with the lemon juice, 1 cup of the Brownulated sugar, the mace, and the cinnamon, blending all the ingredients well.

5. **Complete the pie:** Unwrap one piece of the dough and place it on a lightly floured work surface. Lightly flour the top of the dough and roll it into an 11-inch round, about $\frac{1}{4}$ to $\frac{1}{8}$ inch thick. Roll from the center of the dough to the outside edges, turning it clockwise, to make a round with an even thickness. Place the rolling pin at one edge of the dough and loosely roll the dough around the pin. Lift the rolling pin to the edge of the pie pan and unroll the dough, pressing it into the bottom and sides of the pan. Using a pastry brush, lightly brush the edges of the bottom crust with water.

6. Fill the pie shell with the apples. *(There will be a heaping amount of fruit in the shell.)* Break 3 tablespoons of butter into $\frac{1}{2}$-inch pieces and distribute them over the apple filling.

7. Unwrap the second piece of dough and roll it out as directed for the bottom crust in Step 5. Cover the apples with the top crust and press the edges of the top and bottom crusts together with your fingers. Trim the edges of the crust with scissors, leaving $\frac{1}{2}$ inch of crust draped over the pie pan. Tuck the dough under to make a high edge and press the ends together with the tines of a fork.

8. With a small knife, cut four small vents in the top crust. With a pastry brush, coat the top crust with the egg wash; sprinkle with the remaining tablespoon of Brownulated sugar; then bake the pie for 20 minutes. The

color of the crust will be a deep, golden brown. Lightly cover the top of the pie with foil and bake 25 minutes more. Transfer the pie to a rack to cool.

SERVICE   Cut the pie into 8 wedges and serve it warm, with a generous dollop of your favorite ice cream.

COOK'S TIP   The pie can be reheated in a 375-degree oven or a single piece can be warmed in the microwave for 30 seconds on high power.

Chocolate Chocolate Chip Banana Ice Cream Cake with Pecan Rum Caramel Sauce

KITCHENWARE

small knife, electric mixer, six 4-inch-wide x 2-inch-deep nonstick springform pans, rack, serrated knife, plastic wrap

PREPARATION TIME

40 minutes

BAKING TIME

10 to 12 minutes

DO-AHEAD

Prepare the cakes early in the day and store them, covered, in the freezer for at least 2 hours before serving.

8 large eggs, separated

1 cup sugar

Pinch of salt

2 cups all-purpose flour

1½ pints chocolate chocolate chip ice cream or your favorite flavor

3 medium bananas, cut into ¼-inch-thick rounds (about 12 slices per banana)

1 recipe Pecan Rum Caramel Sauce (recipe follows)

1. Preheat the oven to 350 degrees.

2. Place the egg yolks in the bowl of the electric mixer fitted with the whip attachment. Beat on medium-high speed until they are thick and a light lemon color, 3 to 4 minutes. Reduce the speed to medium and add the sugar in a steady stream, ¼ cup at a time. Increase the speed to medium-high and beat the batter until it is pale yellow and forms ribbons when the whip is lifted from the center of the batter, 3 to 4 minutes. Transfer the batter to the large bowl. Rinse out and dry the mixing bowl and the beaters. *(They must both be perfectly clean and dry or the egg whites won't beat properly.)*

3. Beat the egg whites with the pinch of salt in the bowl of the electric mixer fitted with the whip attachment until they form soft peaks, 3 to 4 minutes. Gently fold the egg whites into the egg yolk batter alternately with the flour, $\frac{1}{4}$ cup at a time. Spoon $\frac{3}{4}$ cup of batter into each of the springform pans and bake the cakes for 10 to 12 minutes, until they spring back when touched in the center. Cool the cakes in the pans on a rack.

4. Remove the ice cream from the freezer and let it soften slightly. While the ice cream is softening, release the sides of the springform pans. Slice each cake into 2 layers with a serrated knife. Remove the top layers, replace the cake bottoms in the pans, and lock the sides of the pans.

5. Arrange 6 slices of banana on top of the bottom layer of each cake. Spread $\frac{1}{2}$ cup of ice cream over the banana and crown each cake with its top layer, placing the flat side up. Cover each cake with plastic wrap and store in the freezer for at least 2 hours before serving.

SERVICE Take the cakes out of the freezer and let them stand at room temperature 20 to 25 minutes before serving. Remove the cakes from the springform pans and invert them onto individual dessert plates. The bottom layer of the cake becomes the top. Spoon 3 heaping tablespoons of hot Pecan Rum Caramel Sauce over each cake.

COOK'S TIPS Any flavor ice cream works well in this cake. For those who are fat conscious, try frozen yogurt. This recipe can also be prepared in a single 8-inch springform pan.

Pecan Rum Caramel Sauce

KITCHENWARE
small heavy-bottomed
saucepan, wooden spoon

**PREPARATION
TIME**
5 minutes

COOKING TIME
7 minutes

DO-AHEAD
The sauce can be made up to
4 days ahead. Cool it and then
store, covered, in the
refrigerator. Reheat the sauce
in the top of a double boiler
before serving.

1 cup packed dark brown sugar

1 cup heavy cream, at room temperature

1 cup broken pecan pieces

1 tablespoon dark rum

1. Combine the sugar and 6 tablespoons water in the saucepan. Cook the mixture over medium heat until it begins to simmer. Reduce the heat to low and slowly cook the sauce, covered, until the syrup has thickened, 3 to 5 minutes.

2. Remove the syrup from the heat and stir in the cream with a wooden spoon. The sauce will become thicker. Cook the sauce, uncovered, over medium-high heat until it has thickened again, about 3 minutes. Stir in the pecans and rum until well blended.

COOK'S TIP Try the warm sauce over puddings, ice cream sundaes, pancakes, or waffles.

Chocolate Chocolate Chip Walnut Brownies

KITCHENWARE
8 x 8-inch baking pan, double boiler, wooden spoon, sifter, small bowl, electric mixer, rubber spatula, rack, fine strainer, plastic wrap

PREPARATION TIME
25 minutes

COOKING TIME
35 to 40 minutes

Five 1-ounce squares unsweetened chocolate
2/3 cup unsalted butter
1 cup all-purpose flour
1 teaspoon baking powder
1/4 teaspoon salt
4 large eggs, at room temperature
2 cups granulated sugar
2 teaspoons pure vanilla extract
1 cup walnut pieces
1/2 cup semisweet chocolate morsels
Garnish: 1/4 cup confectioners' sugar

1. Preheat the oven to 350 degrees. Butter and flour the baking pan.

2. Place the unsweetened chocolate and the butter in the top of a double boiler over medium heat. Gently simmer the mixture, uncovered, stirring occasionally with a wooden spoon, until the chocolate melts, about 5 minutes. Remove the chocolate from the heat and cool.

3. Sift the flour, baking powder, and salt together in the bowl. Set aside.

4. In the large bowl of the electric mixer fitted with the whip attachment, beat the eggs and granulated sugar together on medium speed until the mixture is thick, pale yellow, and forms a ribbon when the beater is lifted from the batter, 3 to 4 minutes. With the mixer on low, blend in the cooled chocolate mixture and the vanilla.

5. Using a rubber spatula, fold the flour mixture, walnuts, and chocolate morsels into the batter until just blended. Pour the batter into the prepared pan and bake 35 to 40 minutes, until a toothpick inserted into the center comes out with a small amount of batter clinging to it.

6. Transfer the pan to a rack and cool the brownies to room temperature for 20 to 30 minutes.

SERVICE Cut the brownies into 2-inch squares and, using a fine strainer, dust them with the confectioners' sugar. Pile the brownies high on a serving tray and cover the tray loosely with plastic wrap until ready to serve.

COOK'S TIPS White chocolate morsels can be substituted for the semisweet chocolate. Remember that the brownies should be moist when removed from the oven.

Citrus Pound Cake with Brandied Raisins

KITCHENWARE
9 x 5 x 3-inch nonstick baking pan, small saucepan, medium bowl, wooden spoon, electric mixer, rack, fine strainer, long spatula

PREPARATION TIME
25 minutes

BAKING TIME
55 to 65 minutes

1 teaspoon plus 1 cup unsalted butter, at room temperature
3 tablespoons brandy
$\frac{1}{2}$ cup golden raisins
2 cups sifted all-purpose flour
1 teaspoon baking powder
1 $\frac{3}{4}$ cups sugar
1 teaspoon pure vanilla extract
1 teaspoon lemon extract
5 eggs, at room temperature
Garnish: $\frac{1}{4}$ cup confectioners' sugar

1. Preheat the oven to 325 degrees. Grease the baking pan with 1 teaspoon of the butter.

2. Bring the brandy and $\frac{1}{3}$ cup water to a simmer over medium heat in the saucepan. Add the raisins, simmer for 1 minute, and remove from the heat. Allow the raisins to steep in the liquid until they are added to the batter in Step 5.

3. Combine the flour and baking powder in the bowl with a wooden spoon and set aside.

4. In the large bowl of the electric mixer fitted with the whip attachment, cream the remaining 1 cup of butter and the sugar together on medium-high speed until the mixture is very light and fluffy, 4 to 5 minutes. Add the vanilla and lemon extracts. Beating on low speed, add the eggs, one at a time, until they are well blended, 3 to 4 minutes.

5. Drain the raisins, discarding the liquid, and blend them into the batter. Continuing to beat on low speed, gradually add the flour mixture until just combined.

6. Spread the batter in the prepared pan and bake for 55 to 65 minutes, until a toothpick inserted in the center comes out clean. Cool the cake in the pan for 10 minutes on the rack. Then invert the cake onto the rack and cool it to room temperature.

SERVICE   If the cake is to be served whole from a buffet, dust the top with the confectioners' sugar sprinkled through a fine strainer while the cake is still on the cooling rack. Transfer the cake with a long spatula to a serving platter.

COOK'S TIPS   If desired, garnish the platter with lemon leaves or fresh flowers and serve with your favorite ice cream. For individual service, cut the cake into serving pieces and top it with ice cream or fresh berries and whipped cream. For a perfect cake, make sure that all the ingredients are at room temperature and that your oven is calibrated properly.

Creamy Cheesecake with Orange and Chocolate

KITCHENWARE

zester, food processor, small bowl, wooden spoon, 8- or 9-inch nonstick springform pan, electric mixer, rubber spatula, baking sheet, rack

PREPARATION TIME

25 minutes

BAKING TIME

I hour

CHILLING TIME

4 hours

DO-AHEAD

The cake can be made a day in advance, refrigerated, and brought back to room temperature before serving.

THE CRUST

10 whole graham crackers
4 tablespoons (½ stick) unsalted butter, melted
2 tablespoons sugar
¾ cup semisweet chocolate morsels

THE FILLING

Three 8-ounce packages cream cheese, at room temperature
¾ cup sugar
4 large eggs, at room temperature
2 tablespoons all-purpose flour
1 teaspoon orange zest
1 teaspoon pure vanilla extract
⅓ cup milk
Garnish: 12 lemon leaves

1. Preheat the oven to 325 degrees.

2. **Make the crust:** Place the graham crackers in the bowl of the food processor fitted with the steel blade and process until they resemble fine crumbs. You should have about 1 cup of crumbs. Combine the cracker crumbs, melted butter, and sugar in the small bowl with a wooden spoon. Press the crumb mixture onto the bottom and about ¾ inch up the sides of the springform pan. Scatter the chocolate morsels over the bottom of the crust. Store the pan in the refrigerator while you prepare the filling.

3. **Make the filling:** Place the cream cheese in the large bowl of the electric mixer fitted with the whip attachment. Beat on medium-high until creamy. Slowly add the sugar and continue beating until the mixture is light and fluffy, about 3 minutes.

4. With the mixer on medium-low, beat in the eggs, one at a time, until each is incorporated into the cheese. Scrape down the sides of the bowl occasionally with a rubber spatula.

5. With the mixer on low, slowly add the flour, orange zest, vanilla, and milk until just combined. Do not overmix. Pour the cheese filling into the prepared crust and bake the cake, set on a baking sheet, for 1 hour. *Do not open the oven to peek.* After 1 hour, turn off the oven and prop the oven door open with a folded potholder; let stand for 20 minutes. Transfer the cake to a rack and cool it completely at room temperature. Remove the sides of the springform pan and chill the cake in the refrigerator for at least 4 hours before serving.

SERVICE   Place the cheesecake on a cake platter and gently slip the lemon leaves under the cake.

COOK'S TIP   Arrange whole fresh strawberries over the top of the cake to make it even more festive.

Intensely Moist Triple Chocolate Cake with Fresh Berries and Cream

KITCHENWARE
chef's knife, 10½-inch-wide x
3½-inch-deep nonstick Bundt
pan, double boiler or glass
bowl, plastic wrap, sifter, small
bowl, electric mixer, rack,
2 long spatulas

**PREPARATION
TIME**
20 minutes

COOKING TIME
35 minutes

9 tablespoons unsalted butter
4 ounces German sweet chocolate, coarsely chopped
3 ounces unsweetened chocolate, coarsely chopped
3 ounces semisweet chocolate, coarsely chopped
½ cup self-rising flour
¾ teaspoon baking powder
½ teaspoon salt
5 large eggs
1¼ cups granulated sugar
¾ cup sour cream
2 teaspoons pure vanilla extract
2 teaspoons cherry liqueur (optional)
Garnishes: 1 teaspoon confectioners' sugar
Fresh Berries and Cream (recipe follows)

1. Preheat the oven to 350 degrees. Grease the Bundt pan with 1 tablespoon of the butter.

2. Cut the remaining 8 tablespoons of butter into 2-inch pieces. Melt the butter and German, unsweetened, and semisweet chocolate using one of the following methods:

❧ Double boiler: Heat the butter and chocolate, partially covered, in the top of a double boiler over medium heat until melted. Blend well, and cool to room temperature.

✻ Microwave: Place the butter and chocolate in a small glass bowl. Cover the bowl well with plastic wrap and microwave on high for 2½ minutes. Uncover the bowl, blend well, and cool to room temperature.

3. Sift the flour, baking powder, and salt together into the small bowl.

4. Put the eggs in the large bowl of the electric mixer fitted with the whip attachment and beat on medium-high speed until they are very thick and light lemon in color, 3 to 5 minutes. Slowly add the granulated sugar, ¼ cup at a time, and continue to beat until the mixture forms ribbons when the whip is lifted from the center of the batter, 3 to 4 minutes.

5. With the mixer on low speed, slowly add the flour mixture until blended. Add the sour cream, vanilla, cherry liqueur, if using, and the melted butter-chocolate mixture. Mix well on low speed to incorporate all the ingredients. Do not overmix.

6. Pour the batter into the prepared Bundt pan and bake for 35 minutes, or until a toothpick inserted in the center comes out clean.

7. Transfer the Bundt pan to a rack and cool for 10 minutes. Remove the pan from the cooling rack and place the cooling rack over the top of the pan. Invert the rack and pan together, holding both sides tightly. The cake will slip out of the pan onto the rack. The bottom of the cake becomes the top.

SERVICE   Dust the top of the cake with confectioners' sugar and, with 2 long cake spatulas, transfer it to a serving platter. Serve the cake with a large dollop of Fresh Berries and Cream, or fill a bowl with the cream and let your guests help themselves.

COOK'S TIP   Chocolate and berries are a great combination.

Fresh Berries and Cream

small knife, colander, electric mixer, serving bowl, spatula or wooden spoon

PREPARATION TIME
20 minutes

DO-AHEAD
Refrigerate the washed berries for 1 hour before serving.

1 quart mixed strawberries, blueberries, and raspberries
1 cup heavy cream
1 teaspoon confectioners' sugar
1 teaspoon pure vanilla extract

1. Stem, wash, and dry the strawberries and cut them into ¼-inch-thick wedges. Wash, stem, and drain the blueberries. Pick through and lightly rinse the raspberries, discarding any that seem mushy. Refrigerate the berries for 1 hour, stored separately.

2. Whip the cream on medium speed in the electric mixer fitted with the whip attachment until it begins to form soft peaks. Add the confectioners' sugar and vanilla and continue to whip the cream until it stands in soft mounds.

SERVICE Spoon the whipped cream into a serving bowl and gently fold the berries into the cream with a spatula or wooden spoon.

COOK'S TIPS Fresh Berries and Cream makes a festive topping for pound cake or ice cream. Add the berries to the whipped cream no more than 15 minutes before serving. If added too soon, the berry juices slowly trickle into the cream, making it lose its shape and become thin. It doesn't matter what kind of berries you use. Depending on seasonal availability, use all three, or two, or just one type of berry.

Orange Chocolate Lace Cookies

KITCHENWARE
zester, large baking sheet,
electric mixer, flat spatula,
rack, fine strainer

**PREPARATION
TIME**
20 minutes

BAKING TIME
5 minutes

1 teaspoon plus 4 tablespoons unsalted butter, at
    room temperature
6 tablespoons all-purpose flour
$\frac{1}{4}$ cup granulated sugar
1 teaspoon pure vanilla extract
2 teaspoons orange zest
1 teaspoon fresh orange juice
2 egg whites
$\frac{1}{3}$ cup chocolate morsels
Garnish: $\frac{1}{4}$ cup confectioners' sugar
6 to 8 $\frac{1}{4}$-inch thick orange wedges

1. Preheat the oven to 450 degrees. Using 1 teaspoon of the
   butter and 2 tablespoons of the flour, butter and lightly
   flour the baking sheet.

2. Place the remaining 4 tablespoons of butter and the granulated sugar together in the large bowl of the electric
   mixer fitted with the whip attachment; beat on medium
   speed until the mixture is completely blended and
   creamy. With the mixer on low, beat in the vanilla and orange zest and juice. Beat in the egg whites, one at a time,
   on medium speed, beating well after each addition.

3. Remove the bowl from the mixer and gently fold the
   chocolate chips and the remaining 4 tablespoons of flour
   into the batter.

4. Drop the batter, 1 teaspoon at a time, onto the prepared baking sheet allowing 1½ inches between cookies. Bake the cookies for about 5 minutes, or until the edges begin to turn golden brown. Allow the cookies to set for 5 minutes at room temperature on the baking sheet. Then, with a flat spatula, remove the cookies to a rack to cool.

SERVICE While the cookies are on the rack, lightly sprinkle them with the confectioners' sugar sifted through a fine strainer. Transfer the cookies with a spatula to a glass or decorative platter and arrange the orange wedges around the rim of the platter.

COOK'S TIP For a tangy taste twist, substitute lemon juice and zest for the orange. These wafers can also be baked in a madeleine pan at 400 degrees for 10 to 12 minutes. Spray the pan with nonstick cooking spray, such as Pam, and dust it with flour before adding the batter. Yield: 12 madeleines.

Peach Yogurt Tea Cake

KITCHENWARE

sharp knife, medium bowl,
colander, sifter, small bowl,
electric mixer, rubber spatula,
10-inch angel food cake
pan, rack

**PREPARATION
TIME**

35 minutes

COOKING TIME

55 to 60 minutes

1 ¾ pounds firm but ripe peaches
3 ¼ cups sugar
1 tablespoon fresh lemon juice
4 ¾ cups all-purpose flour
2 ½ teaspoons baking powder
2 ½ teaspoons baking soda
¾ teaspoon salt
2 teaspoons ground cinnamon
1 teaspoon ground ginger
1 ¼ cups (2 ½ sticks) unsalted butter
5 large eggs
2 ½ cups yogurt
1 tablespoon pure vanilla extract
Garnish: Lemon leaves

1. Slice the peaches in half and remove the pits. Cut each half into ⅛-inch-thick slices, then cut each slice in half. Transfer the peaches to the medium bowl and toss them with ½ cup of the sugar and the lemon juice. Cover and set the bowl aside for 30 minutes. Then drain the peaches in a colander, discarding the juices.

2. Preheat the oven to 350 degrees.

3. Sift the flour, baking powder, baking soda, salt, cinnamon, and ginger together into the small bowl and set it aside.

4. Place the butter and the remaining 2¾ cups sugar in the large bowl of the electric mixer. Beat on medium speed until fluffy, about 5 minutes. With the mixer on medium-low, slowly add the eggs, one at a time, beating well after each addition. Scrape down the sides of the bowl often with a rubber spatula.

5. Increase the mixer speed to medium, add the yogurt and vanilla, and beat until well combined. Add the flour mixture and beat just enough to incorporate the ingredients. Fold the peaches into the batter and spoon the batter into the angel food cake pan. Bake the cake until a toothpick inserted in the center comes out clean, 55 to 60 minutes. Allow the cake to cool on a rack for 10 minutes, then flip it out onto the rack to cool completely.

SERVICE Cut the cake in half, top to bottom. Place one half on a cake stand or platter. Cut the remaining cake into 1½-inch-thick slices and arrange in overlapping slices in front of the whole piece. Garnish the sides of the platter with lemon leaves.

COOK'S TIP Pears, plums, or apricots can be substituted for the peaches.

CHAPTER 7

All-Occasion Drinks

Banana Strawberry Rum Smoothie

Try this when you have a craving for a nourishing "afternoon snack" that is definitely not on Weight Watchers. But don't expect to go back to work after you feel the punch of the rum. Save this one for a lazy Sunday afternoon.

KITCHENWARE
small knife, blender

PREPARATION
TIME
5 minutes

1 ½ cups banana strawberry yogurt
¾ cup strawberry sorbet
2 medium bananas, quartered
3 ounces light rum
Garnish: 2 whole medium strawberries with stems

Combine the yogurt, sorbet, and bananas in a blender. Blend until smooth. Add the rum and blend for 2 seconds.

SERVICE Pour the smoothie into two chilled 8-ounce glasses and garnish each one with a whole strawberry.

Mocha Brandy Night Cap

The perfect end to a gastronomic repast, the icing on the cake, the guarantee that you and your guests will be fasting for the next two weeks, this nightcap is an unfailing promise that your company will go home flashing big smiles of contentment.

KITCHENWARE
blender

PREPARATION TIME
5 minutes

½ ounce brandy
½ cup Bailey's Irish Cream
½ ounce Kahlúa
One 4-ounce scoop mocha ice cream
Garnish: Dark chocolate morsels

Combine all the ingredients except the garnish in a blender. Blend well and pour into a single old-fashioned glass.

SERVICE Garnish the drink with the chocolate morsels.

Steaming Spicy Bull Shot

This "hot toddy" is the perfect answer to a bone-chilling afternoon at a football game or a last run down the slopes. The combination of hot bouillon and spice has the unique effect of waking you up and making you nod off at the same time.

KITCHENWARE
medium saucepan, strainer, small bowl, metal spoon

COOKING TIME
5 minutes

8 ounces beef bouillon
$\frac{1}{4}$ teaspoon well-drained bottled white horseradish
1 dash Worcestershire sauce
1 dash Tabasco sauce
Juice of 1 small lemon
3 ounces vodka, at room temperature
Garnish: Two $\frac{1}{8}$-inch-thick slices lemon

1. the bouillon and horseradish in the saucepan and heat over medium heat until the bouillon begins to simmer. Simmer for 1 minute.

2. Strain the bouillon into a small bowl, add the Worcestershire sauce, Tabasco, lemon juice, and vodka, and stir well. Reheat the bouillon over very low heat if it has lost its steam.

SERVICE Pour the steaming bull shots into two mugs. Garnish each one with a slice of lemon.

Thanksgiving Nonalcoholic Cranberry Punch

The tartness of cranberries and the smokiness of oranges studded with cloves combine to make a punch that is the perfect opening for both grown-ups and offspring before the Thanksgiving feast. If the over-21 guests prefer a little alcoholic tingle in their drink, divide the punch in half and add brandy or vodka for the big guys.

KITCHENWARE
small knife, 4- to 6-cup gelatin mold, baking sheet, large saucepan, strainer, large glass bowl, punch bowl

BAKING TIME
30 minutes

COOKING TIME
20 minutes

4 oranges, halved
32 whole cloves
2½ quarts cranberry juice
1½ quarts fresh orange juice
¼ cup fresh lemon juice
½ cup superfine sugar
1 teaspoon ground cinnamon
1 ring of ice made in a round gelatin mold
1 quart tonic water
Garnish: 10 thin orange slices, halved

1. Preheat the oven to 400 degrees.

2. Stud each orange half with 4 whole cloves. Place the oranges on the baking sheet, skin side up, and bake them for 30 minutes.

3. Heat the cranberry, orange, and lemon juices with the sugar and cinnamon in the saucepan over medium heat. Add the baked oranges and simmer for 20 minutes. Do not allow the mixture to boil. Remove the saucepan from the heat.

4. Squeeze the juice from the orange halves into the punch and discard the oranges. Strain the punch into the glass bowl and cool it to room temperature.

5. Just before serving, unmold the ice ring into the punch bowl. Add the tonic to the punch and pour it over the ice.

SERVICE   Scatter the orange slices over the punch. Place punch cups or mugs around the bowl and let guests help themselves.

Velvety Holiday Eggnog

Rich, velvety eggnog is the perfect potion to serve before brunch, on a frosty afternoon, or as a nightcap after supping on holiday leftovers. If you are serving eggnog before a Thanksgiving or Christmas dinner, make a batch without alcohol for the underage visitors.

KITCHENWARE
electric mixer with 2 bowls, metal spoon

PREPARATION TIME
10 minutes

6 large pasteurized eggs, separated (see Note)
¾ cup superfine sugar
1 ½ cups brandy
½ cup rum
3 cups milk
5 cups heavy cream
Garnish: Grated nutmeg

1. Place the egg yolks and sugar in the bowl of the electric mixer fitted with the whip attachment and beat until they are thick and lemon colored. Beat in the brandy, rum, milk, and heavy cream.

2. Place the egg whites in another mixer bowl. Using very clean beaters, beat until they form soft peaks. Do not overbeat the egg whites, or they will be difficult to incorporate into the eggnog base. Gently fold the egg whites into the yolk mixture until smooth.

SERVICE Pour the eggnog into 4-ounce mugs and sprinkle each portion with nutmeg.

Note: If you are not certain that the eggs are pasteurized, slowly heat the yolks in the top of a Pyrex or stainless-steel double boiler until they just coat the back of a metal spoon.

Fresh Produce Availability Chart

PRODUCE	SEASONS AVAILABLE
Apples	Spring, summer, fall, winter
Artichoke	Summer
Asparagus	Spring, summer
Beans	
Fava	Summer
Green	Summer, fall
Kidney	Summer
Wax	Summer, fall
Beets	Summer, fall, winter
Belgian endive	Fall, winter, spring
Blueberries	Summer
Broccoli	Summer, fall
Brussels sprouts	Summer, fall, early winter
Cabbage	
Green	Spring, summer, fall, winter
Red	Spring, summer, fall, winter
Cantaloupe	Summer
Carrots	Summer, fall
Cauliflower	Summer, fall
Celery	Summer, fall
Celery root	Summer, fall, winter
Corn on the cob	Summer, fall
Cucumber	Summer, fall
Eggplant	Summer, fall
Garlic	Summer, fall
Grapefruit	Spring, summer, fall, winter
Herbs	Spring, summer, fall
Leek	Summer, fall, winter
Lettuce	
Arugula	Spring, summer, fall
Boston	Summer, fall
Boston (hydroponic)	Spring, summer, fall, winter
Escarole	Summer, fall
Iceberg	Summer
Leaf	Spring, summer, fall
Radicchio	Summer, fall
Romaine	Summer, fall

PRODUCE	SEASONS AVAILABLE
Mushrooms	Spring, summer, fall, winter
Nectarines	Spring, summer
Onions (yellow, red)	Spring, summer, fall, winter
Scallions	Summer, fall
Spanish	Summer, fall, winter
Oranges	Spring, summer, fall, winter
Parsley	Summer, fall
Parsnips	Summer, fall, winter
Peaches	Spring, summer
Peppers (all types)	Summer, fall
Plums	Spring, summer
Potatoes	Spring, summer, fall, winter
Pumpkin	Fall
Radishes	Spring, summer, fall
Raspberries	Summer
Rhubarb	Spring, summer
Shallots	Spring, summer, fall, winter
Snowpeas	Summer, fall
Spinach	Summer, fall
Squash (all types)	Summer, fall
Strawberries	Summer, fall
Swiss chard	Summer, fall
Tomatoes	
Beefsteak	Summer, fall
Cherry	Summer, fall
Grape	Summer, fall
Greenhouse	Spring, summer, fall, winter
Italian (plum)	Summer, fall
Turnips	Summer, fall, winter
Zucchini	Summer, fall

Techniques

BLANCH

Bring 5 quarts of water to a boil in a large saucepan or stockpot with 1 teaspoon salt. Add the vegetable and boil for 4 minutes, until just tender. Drain the vegetable in a colander. This technique can be used to blanch a variety of vegetables, including green beans, broccoli, and cauliflower.

BRAISE

Sear and brown seasoned meats, such as beef or lamb, in a large, heavy sauté pan or skillet over high heat. Transfer the meat to a heavy Dutch oven, add liquid as indicated in the recipe, and cook, covered, in a 325-degree oven until the meat is tender.

BUTTERFLY

Cut open but not through and spread apart a boneless leg of lamb or a shrimp. Visualize the wings of a butterfly open in flight—thus, "to butterfly."

CARAMELIZE ONIONS

Cut the onions in a uniform medium dice. Heat oil in a nonstick pan or a heavy-bottomed skillet. Add the onions when the oil is hot. The onions should sizzle, not splatter. To brown, lower the heat and continue cooking, stirring with a wooden spoon, until the sugar in the onions begins to caramelize and the color of the onions becomes a deep brown. Caramelize shallots, red onions, and leeks using the same technique.

CARAMELIZE SUGAR

Sugar is caramelized when it is melted into a deep golden to brown syrup. Combine 1 cup of granulated sugar with $\frac{1}{4}$ cup water in a heavy-bottomed saucepan. Stir well with a wooden spoon until the sugar and water reach a sandy consistency. Place the saucepan over medium heat. As the sugar melts, wash down the sides of the pan with a slightly wet pastry brush. As the sugar heats, it will change in color from amber to a deep brown. Do not stir the sugar during the cooking process.

CLARIFY BUTTER

Heat 6 tablespoons of unsalted butter in a small saucepan over medium heat. When the butter has completely melted, remove it from the heat and let it stand a few minutes, allowing the milk solids to settle at the bottom. Skim the butterfat from the top, making sure not to disturb the solids on the bottom of the saucepan. The butterfat is the clarified butter, which can be reserved in a container and refrigerated for later use.

EGG WASH

Beat 1 egg yolk with 1 teaspoon water or heavy cream.

FOLD

Combine an ingredient of a light consistency, such as beaten egg whites or whipped cream, into a denser mixture, such as a cake batter, using a rubber spatula. Add the lighter mixture to the top of the denser mixture $\frac{1}{4}$ cup at a time. Gently incorporate the lighter mixture with an up-and-over circular motion, slowly rotating the bowl.

GRATE GINGER

Trim and peel the ginger with a paring knife. Place a box grater on a sheet of plastic wrap and rub the ginger across the fine side of the grater. Discard any fibrous outer threads.

KERNEL CORN

Remove the husks and silk threads from the ears of corn. Cut off one end of the stalk to create a flat surface. Stand the corn vertically on a work surface. With a medium sharp knife, cut down vertically along the cob, releasing the kernels of corn. Turn and cut the corn until all the kernels have been removed.

KNEAD

Work the dough with the palms of the hands and fingertips on a lightly flour-dusted work surface to develop the gluten, which is the protein in dough. Lift and turn the dough while kneading, dusting the work surface with more flour as needed to prevent the dough from sticking. Kneading gives the dough elasticity and aids in obtaining even rising and fine texture.

PEEL AND SEED A TOMATO

Remove the core of the tomato with a small sharp knife. Make an X on the bottom of the tomato, cutting just through the skin. Put the tomato in a saucepan of boiling water for 50 seconds; then immediately shock it in cold water. The skin will slip off easily. Cut the tomato in half horizontally. Squeeze each half lightly, allowing the seeds to drop from the tomato. Lightly rinse out the center of the tomato halves.

PURÉE

Reduce a food, such as a vegetable, sauce, or soup, to a uniform smooth consistency in a food processor fitted with the steel blade or in a blender.

ROAST BELL PEPPERS

Roast the peppers for 10 to 12 minutes under the broiler element of an electric range or for 8 to 10 minutes over a gas flame, watching the peppers carefully to make sure they do not burn. Turn the peppers often to uniformly blacken or char the skin. Cool the peppers and peel the skin.

ROAST GARLIC

Preheat the oven to 350 degrees. Place a 12 × 12-inch piece of foil on a work surface. Slice and discard about $\frac{1}{4}$ inch from the top of an unpeeled head of garlic and place the garlic in the center of the foil. Coat the garlic well with 2 teaspoons of extra virgin olive oil. Fold the edges of the foil over to make a sealed package. Place the garlic on a small baking sheet and bake for 45 to 60 minutes, until the flesh of the garlic is very soft.

Remove the foil package from the oven and allow the garlic to cool slightly. Carefully press down at the base of the garlic to squeeze the softened cloves out of their skins. Roasted garlic can be made up to 4 days ahead and stored, covered, in the refrigerator. Bring it to room temperature before using. Yield: about 2 tablespoons.

SEAR

Cook the exterior of food, such as a steak or roast, in a pan over high heat on top of the stove to brown and flavor the surface of the meat and seal in the juices.

SIMMER

Cook food or liquid just below the boiling point.

TRUSS

Tie a chicken, turkey, or game bird with medium-weight white string to preserve its shape and promote even cooking.

ZEST CITRUS

The zest of the fruit is the colored skin of the rind. Set a piece of plastic wrap on a work surface. Set a box grater on top of the plastic. Place the skin of the fruit vertically against the side of the grater, and scrape downward. Be careful not to remove the bitter white pith under the skin. Fruit can also be zested with a paring knife or a flat zester, a tool made specifically for this purpose.

Kitchenware

COOKWARE

6-INCH NONSTICK SKILLET (SMALL)

9-INCH NONSTICK SKILLET (MEDIUM)

12-INCH NONSTICK SKILLET (LARGE)

1-QUART NONSTICK SAUCEPAN (SMALL)

3-QUART NONSTICK SAUCEPAN (MEDIUM)

5-QUART NONSTICK SAUCEPAN (LARGE)

1½-QUART NONSTICK SAUTÉ PAN (SMALL)

5-QUART NONSTICK SAUTÉ PAN (MEDIUM)

8-QUART STOCKPOT

5-QUART STIR-FRY PAN

LARGE NONSTICK ROASTER

STAINLESS-STEEL DOUBLE BOILER

BAKEWARE

6-CUP NONSTICK MUFFIN TIN

12-CUP NONSTICK MUFFIN TIN

24-CUP NONSTICK MINI-MUFFIN TIN

NONSTICK LOAF PAN

2 NONSTICK BAKING SHEETS

2 NONSTICK BAKING PANS

TWO 9-INCH ROUND NONSTICK CAKE PANS

9-INCH NONSTICK SPRINGFORM PAN

QUICHE PAN

SET OF 3 MIXING BOWLS

RAMEKINS

TAPERED ROLLING PIN

PASTRY BRUSH

COOLING RACK

MEASURING CUPS

MEASURING SPOONS

1-QUART LIQUID MEASURE

FLOUR SIFTER

STRAINERS, ASSORTED SIZES

KNIVES

3½-INCH PARING KNIFE

4½-INCH PARING KNIFE

8-INCH CARVING KNIFE

10-INCH SLICER

CHEF'S KNIFE

SHARPENING STEEL

KNIFE BOX

SET OF STEAK KNIVES

SMALL APPLIANCES

TEA KETTLE

4-CUP COFFEEMAKER

12-CUP COFFEEMAKER

COFFEE GRINDER

JUICER

WAFFLE IRON

4-SLICE TOASTER

FOOD PROCESSOR (WITH GRATER AND SHREDDER)

ELECTRIC MIXER (WITH WHISK, BEATER, AND
DOUGH HOOK ATTACHMENTS)

ELECTRIC CAN OPENER

FOOD MILL

ACCESSORIES

COLANDER

WOK

FONDUE SET

PEPPER MILL

SALT SHAKER (OR MILL)

CARVING BOARD

WOODEN SPOONS, ASSORTED SIZES

SPATULAS (RUBBER AND METAL)

MEAT FORK

SLOTTED SPOON

SOUP LADLE

BULB BASTER

WHISKS, ASSORTED SIZES

GARLIC PRESS

VEGETABLE PEELER

CORER

TIMER

INSTANT MEAT THERMOMETER

DEEP-FAT THERMOMETER

CAKE TESTER

SALAD SPINNER

KITCHEN SHEARS

BARBECUE SET

PASTRY BAG

COOKIE CUTTERS

ZESTER

DISH TOWELS

HIS AND HERS APRONS

4 OVEN MITTS

4 POTHOLDERS

SET OF STORAGE BOWLS (FOR FREEZER
    AND/OR REFRIGERATOR)

INDEX